RAMBLIN'
ROBOTS

RAMBLIN' ROBOTS

BUILDING A BREED OF
MECHANICAL BEASTS

INGRID WICKELGREN

A VENTURE BOOK
FRANKLIN WATTS
A DIVISION OF GROLIER PUBLISHING
NEW YORK ▪ LONDON ▪ HONG KONG ▪ SYDNEY
DANBURY, CONNECTICUT

TO MY MOTHER,
THE PERFECT ROLE MODEL
&
TO MY FATHER,
MY WELLSPRING OF OPTIMISM
AND SELF-CONFIDENCE

Cover and Interior Design by Molly Heron
Photographs copyright ©: Cybermotion Inc.: p. 10; Reuters/
Bettmann: p. 12; The Bettmann Archive: pp. 16, 20, 33, 79; The
Computer Museum: p. 18; Library of Congress: pp. 23, 51;
Reprinted with the permission of SRI International, Menlo Park,
CA: pp. 26, 46; Maryland State Fire Marshall: p. 31; NASA: p. 34;
Larkin, Meeder & Schweidel Inc.: p. 38; University of Chicago/
Matthew Gilson: p. 42; Hall of Science Foundation, Schenectady,
NY: p. 57; Odetics, Inc.: p. 59; The Leg Laboratory/Marc H.
Raibert: pp. 69, 72, 75; Artificial Intelligence Laboratory,
Massachusetts Institute of Technology: pp. 92, 113; Bruce Frisch:
pp. 93, 96; Kenneth S. Espen Schied, Roger D. Quinn, Randall D.
Beer, Hillel J. Chiel, Roy Ritzmann, Case Western University:
pp. 104, 105.

Library of Congress Cataloging-in-Publication Data

Wickelgren, Ingrid.
    Ramblin' robots: building a breed of mechanical beasts/by
Ingrid Wickelgren.
        p.   cm.
    Includes bibliographical references and index.
    Summary: Examines the evolution of robotics and the efforts
of scientists to develop robots with the abilities of various
animals.
    ISBN 0-531-11301-9 (lib. bdg.)   ISBN 0-531-15829-2 (pbk.)
    1. Robotics—Juvenile literature.   2. Robots—Juvenile
literature.   [1. Robotics   2. Robots.]   I. Title.
    TJ211.2.W53   1996   95-48767
    629.8'92—dc20   CIP   AC

ACKNOWLEDGMENTS

The author wishes to thank Robert Langreth for his expert advice, and for his support and patience during the preparation of this manuscript.

She is also grateful to the following people for donating their time to answer her many questions, and for reading over and checking portions of this book: John Bares, Randall Beer, Pete Bonasso, Hillel Chiel, Tom Dean, Kenneth Espenschied, Cynthia Ferrell, Ken Fisher, Anita Flynn, Robert Full, Robert Kelley, Marc Raibert, Roy Ritzmann, Reid Simmons, and Steven Shafer.

CONTENTS

INTRODUCTION
What Is a Robot?
9

CHAPTER 1
Road to the First Robot
15

CHAPTER 2
Caution: Robots at Work
28

CHAPTER 3
Mobile Robots and Intelligence
41

CHAPTER 4
Electronic Athletes:
Catching up with Nature
54

CHAPTER 5
Raibert's Running Robots
66

CHAPTER 6
Creepy Secrets from Nature
78

CHAPTER 7
Bugbots, Moondozers, and Other
Simpleminded Machines
86

CHAPTER 8
Robots with Nerve
98

CHAPTER 9
Robot Evolution:
Can Bugbots Breed Humanoids?
108

Appendix: Robot Resources
117

Glossary
119

Source Notes
126

Bibliography
135

Index
140

WHAT IS A ROBOT?

One scoots along the ocean floor searching for buried treasure. Another drills a hole in a patient's head. A third gallops down a hall like a headless metallic horse. A fourth patrols a museum every night. What are these creatures? They're robots, of course.

The term *robot* is used to describe an astounding variety of machines. Different robots have different skills, shapes, sizes, ways of operating, and levels of intelligence. So what on earth is a robot?

The only official definition of a robot in the English language[1] comes from the Robotic Industries Association (RIA). The RIA says a robot is a "reprogrammable, multifunctional machine designed to manipulate materials, parts, tools or specialized devices, through variable programmed motions for the performance of a variety of tasks." In other words, robots are machines that can be programmed to do a specific job, such as moving an object or making something, and then be reprogrammed to do a different job.

Checking out the art: In the Los Angeles County Museum of Art, a robot named SR2 patrols a gallery for polluted air that could damage the paintings.

To be programmable, robots must have a computer brain. That brain distinguishes robots from machine tools, which can only perform one job. A machine tool that stamps out holes in metal parts, for example, cannot be "taught" to spray paint. The ability to *move* is what distinguishes robots from computers, which don't have moving parts.

PARTS OF A ROBOT

The RIA's definition includes a huge variety of programmable devices. All of these devices have four main parts: a body, a brain, brawn, and sensors. Robots may have torsos, arms, and legs like people do. The bodies of other robots look like cylinders on wheels or large, electronic ants. The "robot pilots" that control some airplanes are mere boxes of wires.

Factory robots typically consist of a central pedestal, an arm with a wrist, and gripper hands. Such robots are just moving arms; the rest of their bodies stay still. Those arms may move and turn in a number of different directions, called *degrees of freedom*. If a robot's arm has six degrees of freedom, the arm can move or rotate in all possible directions. Often, the arm has a gripper or another tool for a "hand." Such a tool is called an *end effector*.

A robot's brain is a computer. The computer carries instructions for the motions a robot is designed to perform, any knowledge or "thinking skills" a robot needs, and a way of interpreting data from sensors.

A robot's sensors receive information from the environment. These sensors are the eyes, ears, nose, and skin of the robot. Like human sensory organs, a robot's sensors send the information they collect to the robot's brain.

The brawn or "muscle" of a robot includes motors as well as a power source, which supplies the motors with the energy they need to run. Some robots have *pneumatic motors*, which are powered by compressed air. Other robots have *hydraulic motors*, which run on high-pressure fluid. Many robots have *electric* motors, which are quieter and more precise than pneumatic or hydraulic motors.

Cᴀɴ-Dᴏ Mᴀᴄʜɪɴᴇꜱ

Robots perform a variety of jobs. Almost all *commercial robots*—robots sold to perform specific tasks— are used in factories. They may spray paint, weld, or pickup, place, and package goods. In hospitals, robots deliver medicines, or help doctors with operations. On farms, they milk cows or shear sheep. Some robots help disabled people by bringing books, toothbrushes, and other objects whenever the people ask for them.

Without coffee breaks, robots labor day and night piecing together the bodies of cars at a factory in Japan.

Robots excel at many jobs that people dislike or find difficult. For example, robots are good at performing boring, repetitious tasks such as sorting objects on an assembly line.

Also, robots can assist in procedures, such as brain surgery, that require a great deal of precision. In addition, robots can work in places that are too dangerous for humans—the bottom of the ocean, the surface of Mars, or inside nuclear power plants.

Redefining Robots

Many scientists see robots as more than workhorses, however. To them, real robots should mirror intelligent life. Most *roboticists* (robot scientists) who work for universities are not trying to build robots to do specific tasks. Instead, they aim to create mobile machines that are intelligent and agile. They would like to create artificial beings that can survive on their own in the unpredictable, real world.

Most commercial robots do not come close to achieving this goal. That's because it takes time for an invention to be developed and produced for commercial use. During that time, laboratory researchers working elsewhere may come up with improvements. It may be years before robots incorporating these improvements make it to the marketplace.

Some roboticists consider the robots that attach fenders to cars or screw lids on jelly jars too stupid to deserve the name "robot." They prefer to limit the term "robot" to their more recent, more sophisticated creations.

Recognizing Robots

This book will define "robot" more broadly than many researchers do. In fact, it will use a definition that is even more general than the one stated by the

RIA. Any machine that an ordinary person might call a robot will be called a robot on these pages.

This more flexible definition jibes with the ideas of Joseph Engelberger, the so-called "father of robotics." "I can't define a robot," Engelberger once said, "but I know one when I see one."[2]

Robot Evolution

The first two chapters of this book will summarize the evolution of robots through the present day. Chapters 3–9 focus on robots of the future—the robots that are being developed in laboratories across the country. The scientists working on these strive to craft the smartest, most agile machines humankind has seen.

Chapter 3 introduces the traditional approach to creating smart robots in which scientists mold machines after humans. Chapters 4–8 describe the efforts of researchers who take an alternative approach: They model robots after animals. Some of these scientists strive to create machines that mimic animal agility. Others copy animal survival skills. Many of the scientists working on these robots try to follow the path of animal evolution, starting with simple skills and then adding more sophisticated smarts after many robot generations.

Chapter 9, the final chapter, tells of an ambitious leap in electronic evolution that may result in the birth of a novel humanlike robot.

CHAPTER 1
ROAD TO THE FIRST ROBOT

According to ancient Greek legend, Hephaestus, the god of fire, makes female figures out of gold and brings them to life. The figures were said to move, speak, and think—helping the god in his work.[1]

For thousands of years, people have fantasized about bringing objects to life. Intelligent, lifelike creations seem both magical and potentially very useful. Humanity's desire for magical toys and intelligent tools that do work for them ultimately spawned the machines we call robots.

MECHANICAL "LIFE"

During the 1700s, inventors used *clockwork* (the technology used to make old-fashioned clocks) to create the first sophisticated animated objects. Clockwork involves connecting wheels, weights, springs, and levers in intricate ways so that a device will perform a precisely timed sequence of motions. The technology was used to create *automatons*, mechanical devices that produce the illusion of life.

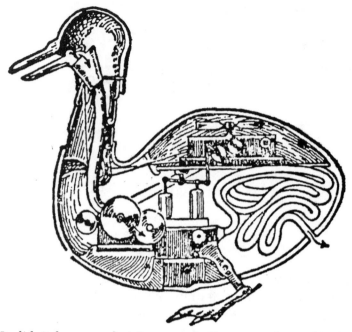

It didn't lay eggs, but Jacques de Vaucanson's mechanical duck did quack, eat grain, and even expel the digested "food."

One of the most celebrated automatons was a mechanical duck built by Jacques de Vaucanson in 1738. Vaucanson's copper duck quacked, walked, bathed, and appeared to eat and drink.[2]

Another famous creation was a boy scribe. Built by the Swiss craftsman Pierre Jacquet-Droz in 1770, the mechanical boy dipped a pen in ink and wrote short messages. Through an elaborate system of wheels and levers, the scribe's hand was able to move in three dimensions and could write up to forty different characters.[3]

WEAVING THOUGHTS

Although automatons looked lifelike and entertained audiences, they were of limited use because they could only perform a rigid set of actions. A machine whose behavior can be easily altered to suit various situations needs a computer.

The history of the computer began, oddly enough, with the world's first automatic weaving loom. Built in 1745 by Jacques de Vaucanson, the maker of the mechanical duck, that loom—and a more advanced loom built by Joseph Marie Jacquard in 1801—used a control system very similar to the one used by the first computers.[4]

The Jacquard loom added a new dimension to the standard weaving loom of the 1700s. To use the standard loom, an operator moved needles through holes in a block of wood to create the desired pattern. In the automatic looms, punched cards controlled the pattern woven by the loom.

The cards were inserted between the needles and the wood. Where a card had holes, needles passed through the card and entered the wood. Where a card had no holes, needles were blocked from entering the wood. In this way, yarn was woven in arrangements specified by the pattern of holes in cards. Weavers could "program" the pattern they wanted by inserting cards in the looms in a particular order.[5]

PUNCHING CARDS

In the 1830s, the automatic loom inspired British mathematician Charles Babbage to develop an idea for a computer that used punched cards to store information. Babbage was the first person to envision a digital computer, the kind of computer we have

This automated loom, built by Joseph Marie Jacquard, was an extremely successful sewing device that resembled the first computers.

today. *Digital computers* store all information, including sounds and pictures, as numbers. They perform tasks by changing one set of numbers into another set. Although Babbage's ideas were brilliant, his vision could not be realized during his lifetime because the technology was not up to the task.[6]

The first working computer arrived in the 1880s. Invented by American statistician Herman Hollerith, the machine read data in the form of punched cards. But the key to its success was the use of *electricity*, the energy carried by tiny charged particles called *electrons*, to count the numbers stored on the cards. The machine did its calculations by passing an electric current along metal contacts made through the holes in the cards. Hollerith's machine performed many jobs for business and government. It saved years of human labor by calculating the U.S. censuses of 1890 and 1900.[7]

Over the next several decades, *electromechanical* tabulators like Hollerith's became faster. They reached peak speed in 1944, when Harvard professor Howard Aiken built Mark I, the first calculator fast enough and sophisticated enough to tackle scientific problems. Because Mark I used electrical switches similar to the switches in today's digital computers, some scientists consider Mark I to be the world's first digital computer.[8]

THE BIRTH OF ELECTRONICS

Electromechanical machines such as Hollerith's and the Mark I depended on moving parts to control counting wheels. As a result, their speed and reliability were limited. By the end of World War II, computer engineers were ready for a new technology.

The technology these computer engineers would adopt had already been in use for two decades to

Try putting this on your desk. The first general-purpose electronic computer, called ENIAC, filled a large room and more.

make radios. It was known as *electronics*, a technology based on the precise control of electric current. In electronics, current is not used to turn on lights or run motors, but as a way of carrying information.

The first electronic device was the *vacuum tube*, a glass tube from which almost all the air has been removed. Inside the tube, various metallic parts produce and help control a beam of electrons, which moves through the tube. In the 1920s, vacuum tubes served as amplifiers in radios. Twenty-five years later, they began new lives as switches. They performed calculations and served as memory units inside computers.

The first general-purpose computer to use vacuum tubes was developed in 1945 by John William Mauchly and John Presper Jr. at the University of Pennsylvania. The computer, which was named *ENIAC* (Electronic Numerical Integrator and Calculator), was designed to use the *decimal system*. This is the same system that you use to count. ENIAC stored each number between 0 and 9, using a ring of 10 vacuum tubes. The number of "on" tubes in a ring represented the digit. For instance, if three tubes out of ten were "on," the digit was "3."[9]

An Electronic Code

Although ENIAC stored information in vacuum tubes, it did not have an electronic program. Instead, programmers laboriously inserted plugs into electrical sockets on a board. Wiring a *plug board* created specific and rigid electrical paths whereby ENIAC would carry out its computations.

By 1947, John von Neumann unveiled *EDVAC* (Electronic Discrete Variable Automatic Computer), which was much more flexible and adaptable than computers that ran rigid plug-board programs. EDVAC could read electronic programs that contained choices or branches among several paths of action.[10]

In addition, EDVAC read and carried out only binary arithmetic, a system that represents numerical values as a string of 1s and 0s. The *binary system* is much better suited to electronic components than the decimal system because a binary digit can be stored by the state of a single electronic component—a "1" indicated that a switch was "on" and a "0" indicated that a switch was "off."[11]

THE TRANSISTOR

As powerful as they were, EDVAC and ENIAC were energy-gobbling monsters. Vacuum tubes are large, generate a lot of heat, and wear out quickly. Any computer that used them required rooms of space, lots of energy, and frequent repairs. They were certainly too big to put into mobile robots.

In 1947, researchers found a way to eliminate the hassles of vacuum tubes. William Shockley and two other American physicists, John Bardeen and Walter Brattain, invented the *transistor*, a tiny device that controls the flow of electric current through a solid material instead of a vacuum.

Like vacuum tubes, transistors can be used as amplifiers or switches inside computers. But the first transistors were about the size of an eraser on the end of a pencil—much smaller than vacuum tubes, which are as big as whole dill pickles. Transistors also give off less heat and use less power than vacuum tubes do.

THE INDUSTRIAL ROBOT

Because of their advantages, transistors began to replace vacuum tubes in the electronic equipment of the 1950s. Among other things, the transistor made possible the development of the first industrial (factory) robots.

The first patent for an industrial robot was granted in 1954 to George C. Devol Jr. He called its computer memory and control system "universal automation" or "unimation." In the 1960s, Devol sold his ideas to Joseph F. Engelberger, who transformed them into robots he called "Unimates."[12]

Unimates were moving arms attached to huge computer brains housed in separate rooms. They were programmed by using a hand-held device to

Armed for duty. A Unimate robot—really, just an arm—picks up and puts down parts in a General Electric factory.

lead the Unimate through the desired motions. At various points in the lesson, a programmer would enter the correct position of the arm in the Unimate's memory. When the robot was ready, it would play back its instructions, adjusting its arm to match the positions stored in its memory.[13]

THE INTEGRATED CIRCUIT

In the early days, a transistor was a separate device fastened to a base that supported an electronic circuit. A circuit's transistors were linked to each other and to other components via wires. Such circuits were a powerful advance over the vacuum-tube circuits, but they had disadvantages. They were still too large for many applications. They were also disorderly, as their wires often wound up in a tangled mess.

To shrink and simplify a circuit, Jack Kilby, an American engineer, and Robert Noyce, an American physicist, invented a way to embed hundreds of transistors inside a paper-thin chip made of a special semiconducting crystal. In 1959, that technique was used to create the first *integrated circuit* (IC), a solid chip imprinted with minute paths and regions through which current flows. Those paths, made of different materials, perform various functions. Tiny metal pathways serve as microscopic wires. Regions of silicon with carefully added impurities act as transistors, controlling the flow of current by amplifying it, changing its nature, or switching its direction.

The first integrated circuits contained all the functions of a conventional circuit but were 1,000 times smaller. Today, ten million transistors can fit on an IC the size of a baseball trading card.[14] Integrated circuits are much smaller, faster, cheaper, and more reliable than conventional circuits. They are the working units inside many of today's electronic devices, including watches, radios, TVs, computers, and, of course, robots. The development of integrated circuits eventually made it possible to provide robots with small computer brains that could be attached to the robots themselves.

Robot Revolution

During the 1970s, robots entered the workplace by the thousands. The robot workforce included Unimates and smaller robots called PUMAs (Programmable Universal Machines for Assembly) made to handle small parts on assembly lines. Such robots revolutionized the auto industry, increasing production and reducing error rates.[15] Although robots now work in many places, automobile plants are still the most common habitat for industrial robots, which now number more than 50,000 in the United States.[16]

Advances in computer technology led to machines that could be said to "think" and respond to their surroundings—to some extent. In 1969, researchers at SRI International (then called the Stanford Research Institute) in Palo Alto, California, built the first robot that could think and respond to the world around it. The birth of that robot, Shakey, began the laboratory tradition of building intelligent mobile robots.

The Imaginary Robot

Science fiction writers imagined artificial creatures long before scientists could create them. In the 1921 play *R.U.R. (Rossum's Universal Robots)* by Czech playwright Karel Capek (pronounced CHOP-ek), an Englishman named Rossum creates a breed of artificial men and women to do the world's work. The artificial people are perfect slaves until they are given emotions, which cause them to hate their human masters. They revolt, wipe out the human race, and start their own intelligent robot society.

R.U.R. stands as a warning to humanity about the potential dangers of creating artificial life-forms. More significantly perhaps, it also introduced Amer-

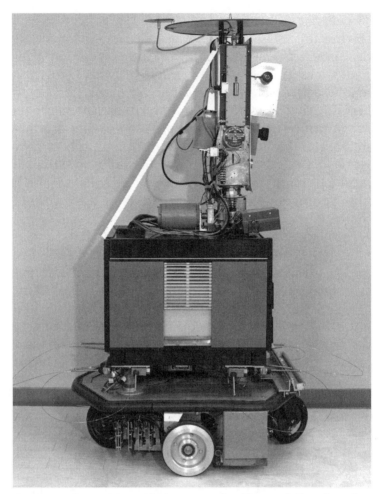

Smart and sensitive. Shakey was the first mobile robot that could think and respond to the world around it.

icans to the word robot. The word comes from the Czech word robota, which means work or forced labor.

As time passed, people began to think of robots less as rebellious slaves than as benevolent machines.

Such notions were encouraged by Isaac Asimov's 1942 science fiction story *Runaround*, which spells out the now-famous Three Laws of Robotics.[17]

1. A robot may not injure a human being, or through inaction, allow a human being to come to harm.
2. A robot must obey the orders given by human beings, except when such orders would conflict with the First Law.
3. A robot must protect its own existence, as long as such protection does not conflict with the First or Second Law.

In the Asimov tradition, the robots portrayed on TV and in movies—for example, DATA of *Star Trek* and R2D2 and C3PO of the *Star Wars* trilogy—are intelligent creatures that obey the rules. And so most people still think of robots as the Greeks thought of Hephaestus's golden girls—as smart, friendly, and capable. In part, those people are right. Robots are reasonably friendly. That's because, as we shall see, they aren't smart enough to disobey.

CHAPTER 2

CAUTION: ROBOTS AT WORK

Glug glug. Nemo, a 6-ton robot, scoots along the bottom of the ocean. Nemo approaches a glass bottle filled with gold coins. People on a ship above see the submerged prize on computer screens that show pictures taken by Nemo's camera "eyes." Someone sends an electrical message through a cable telling Nemo to pick up the bottle. The robot does so gently, so as not to break it.[1]

Nemo's job is to recover gold and interesting objects that long ago sunk to the ocean floor with submerged ships, planes, and other craft. Like a puppet, Nemo's every move is controlled by a person. The undersea robot is connected to its operator by a cable, which transmits electrical messages that the operator types into a computer.[2]

COPING WITH CHAOS

Nemo is in a class of robots called "puppet robots."[3] The robot's movements are directed, moment by moment, by a person. Like all of today's employed robots, Nemo is not smart enough to work in complex, ever-changing places, such as oceans, on its own. Robot scientists are trying to make robots that are more flexible and independent. Those efforts are described in the next chapter and in the rest of this book.

This chapter sketches the strategies used to operate today's working robots, which are unable to deal with the chaos and uncertainty of the real world. As we shall see, each of these control strategies has some disadvantages.

There are three main control strategies for working robots. The first, used by puppet robots, relies on control by humans, who are smart enough to handle any situation that arises. A second strategy, used for most stationary robots, involves placing robots in structured settings where conditions will change very little. The third strategy, used for the mobile robots that we'll call "coddled *rovers*," employs physical structures, such as wires, or maps programmed in robots' brains, to guide the robots through specific workplaces.

PUPPET ROBOTS

Puppet robots are controlled by people tilting joysticks, pushing buttons, dragging computer mice, giving verbal orders, or gesturing with electronic gloves. However a command is given, that command is carried to the robot in one of two ways: It either travels through a cable or through the air via radio signals.

Robots that respond to radio waves are called remote-control robots or *telerobots*. Telerobots have paced the bottoms of oceans, captured suspected criminals, stepped into active volcanoes, and explored outer space.

Deep-sea Diving

Puppet robots may dive into oceans for reasons other than recovering lost treasures. In the 1970s, they welded underwater pipes, cut metal, and tightened bolts for companies exploiting undersea oil fields. Today, they help scientists find previously undiscovered life-forms in the deep ocean, study undersea volcanoes, and survey coral reefs. A robot named Jason dove down to the bottom of the Gulf of California to study hot vents (cracks) in the ocean floor.[4]

Nemo, Jason, and almost all undersea robots receive instructions and send data through long tethers that extend up to human drivers on ships. Driving these robots is difficult and tedious. First of all, an operator must drive almost blind, since cameras on the robots provide only short-range views of the landscape. In addition, expeditions are often long, and robot puppeteers find it hard to concentrate on tilting a joystick for hours on end. Because of such difficulties, puppet robots often crash or get stuck in tight spots.

Nabbing a Suspect

In 1993, a remote-control robot helped Maryland police capture a murder suspect. Controlled by radio waves sent by a police officer a safe distance away, the 3-foot-high (1-m-high) robot, called RMI, opened an apartment door with its metallic claw and scanned the scene with its TV-camera eye. Looking through that eye, the officer in charge saw the suspect hiding under a pile of clothes and directed the robot to shoot water from its water cannon. The blast stunned the suspect, and the police ran in for the capture.[5]

The remote-control six-wheeler, RMI, isn't always sun-bathing. Using its camera-eye, the robot once helped police spot a murder suspect, who was hiding under a pile of clothes in an apartment.

Despite that stunning success, RMI has limited use as a crook-catcher. Moving a puppet robot fast enough to follow a moving human is nearly impossible. In most situations, a crook could easily escape a remote-control robot.

Roaming a Volcano

In the summer of 1994, an eight-legged robot named Dante II marched more than 590 feet (180 m) down into the steep, rocky crater of Alaska's Mount Spurr volcano. Inside the volcano, the robot took the temperature of volcanic gases and shot movies of the treacherous landscape. Unfazed by the hazardous conditions, the spiderlike robot collected more data than any human scientist could have.

Dante was controlled by scientists stationed 81 miles (130 km) away in Anchorage, Alaska. Operators watched Dante's movements on a computer monitor. They also could view the scene around Dante in 3-D using stereo glasses. That mode of operation, called *telepresence*, creates a sense of being onboard the robot.[6]

Dante II's success was due, in large part, to its own intelligence. Although human controllers told the robot which direction to go, Dante had the smarts to skirt boulders and other obstacles on its own.

Exploring Space

In the 1970s, Soviet scientists drove the first remote-control robot, Lunakhod, on the moon. Controlling a moon rover is difficult because radio messages take three seconds to travel from Earth to the moon. This means that a robot on the moon reacts to instructions from earthlings 3 seconds after they are sent.

*Perched atop a carpet of snow,
Dante II is about to descend
into the steep, steamy crater of
Mount Spurr, a volcano in Alaska.*

To experience the delay, walk across a room while counting to three between each step!

Now, a team of Russian and American scientists are testing a telerobot, called the Mars Rover, that they plan to drive on Mars in 1998. But they have a problem. A radio message takes 8 to 40 minutes to make the trip from Earth to Mars and back. That delay could mean disaster for the Mars Rover. Say the rover is near a Martian cliff. A message to "back up" is sent. While the message is making its way to Mars, the robot steps over the cliff.

In this artist's conception, the Mars Rover is collecting rocks and other souvenirs from the Red Planet.

To avoid mishap, scientists will move the six-wheeled Mars Rover very slowly when it first lands on the Red Planet. However, they hope to rev up the rover later in the mission using telepresence. Here's how: As the rover rolls around Mars, it will stop frequently to take pictures. It will send those pictures to Earth, where computers will assemble them into large, 3-D views of Mars. Peering through stereo glasses at those views, operators will see realistic pictures of the robot's surroundings, including distant hazards. With such views, operators hope to safely move the rover farther with each command.

However, telepresence can't completely overcome the problems of time delay. Seeing in the distance can't protect the rover from a boulder that's about to crush it, or from sinking into a sandpit that it's standing on. Planetary rovers need the ability to react to nearby hazards on their own because messages from Earth may reach them too late.

STATIONARY ROBOTS

There's not a human in sight. But, as usual, Plant 41 of Pratt & Whitney Canada is making parts for aircraft engines. An electronic signal zips to a huge crane gliding along steel tracks. The crane lifts a big chunk of metal off a high shelf and moves it down to the warehouse floor. The crane lays its burden on a driverless robotic cart, which takes it to robots that whittle it into shape.[7]

The robots at Plant 41 are fast, efficient, and accurate. So are thousands of other factory robots, which spray paint, weld, pour poisons, and place parts on everything from cars to jelly jars. Factory robots are excellent employees. They don't get sick or take coffee breaks—and they don't need human guidance. Their computer brains are programmed to lead them through the motions needed to complete specific tasks.

However, factory robots are far from independent. Deaf, dumb, and blind, most are so unaware of their surroundings they must work in static settings that have been built especially for them. If something in a factory robot's surroundings unexpectedly changes, the robot will probably be unable to do its job.

For example, a robot that screws light bulbs into sockets works fine when a socket is where it is supposed to be. But say a socket has been moved. The robot is then likely to screw a bulb into the empty space that the socket usually occupies.

Bombs Away!

Factory-type robots are now working in places other than factories. In laboratories, modified factory robots handle the fragile materials used to make everything from computer chips to medicines. At Sandia National Laboratories, a modified factory robot is doing the hazardous job of separating the radioactive, central "pit" of a nuclear warhead from the explosives that surround it. By performing this chore, a step in the disassembly of nuclear weapons, the robot saves human workers from exposure to harmful radiation.

Robodoc

Factory-type robots also work in hospitals. The drilling technology used by many factory robots is now being used to drill holes in human hip bones. Robodoc, a robot hip surgeon developed by Integrated Surgical Systems of Sacramento, California, follows orders, doesn't faint at the sight of blood, and is very precise. A human can't move a hand exactly 0.11 inch (2.8 mm). Robodoc can.[8]

To do its job, Robodoc—really, just a wand tipped by a tiny propeller—needs a map and a plan from a human doctor. After scanning X rays of a patient's leg into Robodoc's computer brain, the doctor uses a mouse to sketch a plan for the surgery. While Robodoc's propeller tunnels into a hip bone, the human surgeon looks on, with one finger on the pause button.[9]

CODDLED ROVERS

Like stationary robots, most mobile robots also live in structured, unchanging environments. The difference, of course, is that mobile robots move—and so they must be able to tolerate a little less structure than stationary robots.

Some mobile robots need wires or other physical structures to know where to go. Others rely on electronic maps programmed into their brains to guide them through specific settings. With a map and some obstacle-avoidance skills, a rover can work in its assigned place. However, it will be utterly lost when confronted with an environment for which it does not have a map.

Mowing Lawns

In 1994, Poulan/WeedEater in Shreveport, Louisiana, unveiled a robot that mows lawns. An owner must bury wires in the ground around a lawn to mark the boundaries for the robot. When the lawn *mobot*, which looks like a big plastic turtle, comes close to a wire, a sensor on the mower picks up sig-

No more mowing. This mobot will roam your yard without you, cutting grass wherever it senses blades that are too tall.

nals from the wire, causing the robot to stop and turn. Within the boundary, the robot roams freely. It senses where the grass is tall and needs trimming, and reflexively stops and turns after bumping into obstacles such as lawn chairs and trees.

Patrolling Buildings

At night, when nobody's around, a robot rolls through the halls of the Los Angeles Museum of Art. The robot, called SR2, is programmed with a map of the particular exhibit it is supposed to patrol.[10] (The robot must be reprogrammed every time an exhibit's layout changes.) Guided by such a map, it uses sensors to detect walls and small obstacles. The robot roams along a preplanned path, sniffing the air for humidity, smoke, and polluting chemicals that could damage artwork.[11]

Nursebot

HelpMate, a robot from Transitions Research Corporation (TRC) in Connecticut, runs errands in another structured setting—a hospital. Programmed with a map of the hospital and specific instructions on where to go, the 4-foot-tall (1.2-m-tall) boxlike robot carries food trays, records, medicine, and supplies to and from various indoor locations. The robot must be reprogrammed when a hospital's layout changes or when it's moved to a new hospital.

Nevertheless, HelpMate is a capable robot. It can operate elevators and, using sensors, can navigate around patients, doctors, and beds. If something gets in Helpmate's way, it stops and says, "My way is blocked. Please remove the obstacle." It repeats itself until someone clears its path.

ROBOT LIBERATION

Commercial robots are evolving to perform more and more tasks on their own. However, these robots are still limited to specific tasks and specific, unchanging places. In laboratories, though, scientists are striving to give robots the skills to wander freely. Researchers are raising robots to "do more and more things with less and less supervision—the way that parents raise their children," says engineer Robert Kelley of Rensselaer Polytechnic Institute in Troy, New York.

A truly independent machine could go many places and do many things that no robot can today. Robots might explore Mars without remote control from humans. Tiny robots might perform surgery from inside a person's bloodstream. Robot cars might drive people wherever they want to go. A robot might someday live on its own in the ocean, probing undersea eruptions and other deep-sea happenings.

To be independent, robots must be both smart and agile. The remaining chapters of this book focus on scientists' attempts to build independent, mobile robots. They explore efforts to create agile robots that move on legs, and mobile robots, both legged and wheeled, that are smart enough to deal with the real world.

MOBILE ROBOTS AND INTELLIGENCE

The octagonal metallic robot ponders the scene: A room in a mazelike "office" is strewn with wads of paper, Styrofoam™ cups, and soda cans. The robot, named CHIP by its creators from the University of Chicago, is going wire to wire against its electronic rivals at the 1994 Mobile Robotics Competition in Seattle, Washington.[1] The robot's mission: To pick up as much trash as possible and put it in the bins located around the office.

"Scanning for trash," says CHIP as little lights on its side blip on and off. The robot's tubular, black eyes angle downward, and it announces, "I see some trash." The robot slowly rolls its way toward a wad of paper, reaches down with its long gripper arm, and grabs the wad. It eventually finds a bin, rolls over to it, and drops the single piece of trash inside. The ordeal takes 14 minutes, way over the 10-minute time limit. But the audience is impressed.

In the finals of the competition, CHIP fares less well. It announces its intentions, but hardly moves at all. At least CHIP has the sense to recognize

Gripping a soda can, CHIP glances at one of its creators, James Firby. The television screen in back shows exactly what CHIP sees through its robot eyes.

ordinary-looking trash. Some of CHIP's rivals can only recognize highly unusual trash—narrow, cardboard boxes that tower over them like skyscrapers. Changing the shape and size of the trash is apparently within contest rules.

CHIP was the only robot that could actually pick up trash: It was the only machine with an arm. The rest of the robots, including the winner, scurried up to trash and pretended to pick it up. Actual trash collecting was considered too difficult for the robots, so judges gave equal points to competitors that "virtually" manipulated the junk in the room.

What It Means to Be Free

Why do grown-up scientists build robots that do such a silly task? They aren't looking for novel ways to pick up after their kids. No, these researchers want to see whose robot is the smartest.

Contest organizers chose the trash task because doing a simple thing in a complex, messy place is a challenge for robots. The scientists' ultimate goal is to create truly independent, or *autonomous*, robots—that is, robots that can deal with the everyday world on their own.

To be truly autonomous, a robot must make its way through everyday landscapes, such as cluttered offices, without wires, trails, or other physical structures set up to help it figure out where to go. It must work without a tether or any other tie to a human puppeteer. An autonomous robot must also be able to get around without having to be reprogrammed for every new, slightly different setting. It must deal with sudden, unforeseen events and situations, from potholes to roller-skating teenagers. The world is full of such surprises.

Robots that deftly handle surprises could hang

out and work in many places that today's robots cannot. They might, for example, maneuver through complex outdoor landscapes such as forests and farms, or do chores in chaotic indoor scenes such as school cafeterias and cluttered bedrooms. They might rescue people from burning buildings, wash dishes, explore Mars, or even pick up trash.

PEOPLE OR ANIMALS?

Scientists have spent decades searching for ways to make truly autonomous robots. As is clear from the robots in the competition, the search is far from over. Although the mobile robots made in university labs are generally smarter, more agile, and more sensitive to their surroundings than commercial robots, they are still very limited in what they can do.

Scientists disagree about the best way to make robots independent. Many researchers in the field of *artificial intelligence* (AI), the science of making smart machines, feel that robots should be built to think abstractly, or reason, like people do. These *traditional AI* researchers are still following the path to making smart machines that was paved back in the 1950s by the pioneers in the field of artificial intelligence.

Other roboticists do not agree with the notions of traditional AI. Instead of trying to make robots reason, these scientists hope that their robots will copy the skills of simpler animals. Their research, which will be detailed in Chapters 4–9, challenges the notion that abstract thought is necessary for robot autonomy. Animal-like agility and simple survival skills, argue these researchers, are the most important skills for independent robots to have.

Meanwhile, traditional AI researchers have stuck to the notion that humanlike abstract thought is crucial to robot autonomy. However, in recent years, many have heeded some of the principles championed by the animal robot pioneers: They give robots simple animal-like behaviors in addition to human-like reasoning skills. We will return to that hybrid approach, which has produced many capable robots, in Chapter 9. This chapter will discuss traditional AI in its pure form and the reasons some researchers chose to retreat from tradition.

Let's Be Reasonable

To make a robot think abstractly, or reason, like a human does, traditional AI researchers need some idea of how humans think. Most of them subscribe to a theory put forth some 40 years ago by AI pioneers Herbert Simon and Allen Newell of Carnegie-Mellon University.

Simon and Newell saw human intelligence as the ability to represent the world with symbols, such as words, equations, and charts, and to use reasoning to manipulate those symbols. Their theory breaks thought into four stages: perception, reasoning, planning, and action. At each stage, a map, or mental picture, of the world is used to decide how to act.[2]

On that theory, traditional AI researchers program robots to first perceive their surroundings and then reason about them in stages. To do this, a robot is given a map of the place it will be exploring. It then reasons about the map and forms a plan that will help it reach its goal. After lots of pondering, the robot acts.

Shakey, a Reasoning Robot

One of the first mobile robots to reason in this way was Shakey, a big box on wheels built in the late 1960s by scientists at SRI International in Palo Alto, California. Named for its wobbly way of moving,

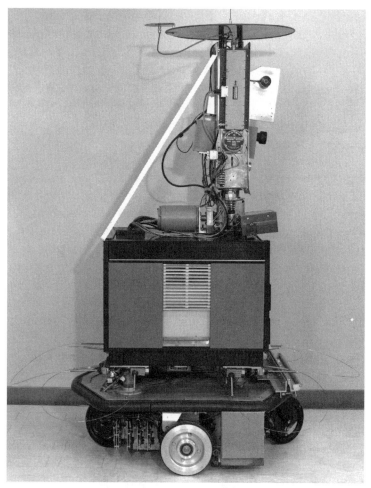

A wobbly box on wheels, Shakey could sense things around it, and could solve problems—but only in a simple world that contained clean walls and a few large, smooth objects.

Shakey used knowledge, logic, and reasoning to solve problems such as how to push a block off a platform that was too high for it to reach and how to stack blocks.

Although Shakey could perform some interesting tricks, it was useless outside its very simple world—a static setting that contained only clean walls and a few large, smooth objects. Why? For one thing, Shakey was very slow. The robot took an hour to find a block and a ramp in a simple scene.[3] It would ponder information from its sensors for minutes at a time before deciding what to do. In the real world, things change much more quickly than Shakey could act.

For another thing, Shakey was programmed to understand only certain scenes and situations. Anything outside of its programmed repertoire would completely confuse it. Shakey could never have understood an office setting with different lighting, dirty walls, or scattered furniture. The robot was confused by such complexities because it did not have a general understanding of the world—what people call *common sense.*

Senses and Common Sense

Nowadays, robots that use Shakey's style of thought are faster than Shakey was, in part because their computer brains are more powerful. However, like CHIP, they can still be slow when confronted with a complex task that requires perception, reasoning, and manipulation. In addition, mobile robots have trouble adapting to a changing world because they have little, if any, common sense.

Common sense involves reacting to the messiness of everyday life. It is not one single insight but lots of little ideas and simple skills. It includes concepts such as "objects that are not supported will fall" and "a person cannot be in two places at once."[4] Common sense is natural to people, but no robots have it—and that is why robots can't get along on their own in the real world.

Why is common sense so hard to "teach" a robot? Because it is hard to teach—period. People don't learn common sense from books, quizzes, and lectures. They learn it from experience with the world—through their eyes, ears, and other sensory organs. People use their senses to construct mental pictures that they use to understand the world.

Seeing Only the Light

Robots can use their senses to construct mental pictures, but those pictures aren't good enough to give them common sense. Why not? Because robot senses aren't very good. One of the biggest handicaps robots have is poor vision.

Robots can't see, at least not the way people see. Robots can be given "eyes" by attaching cameras to their computer brains. What they "see" is just a grid of numbers, which correspond to values of lightness and darkness. As a result, computers can find places where lightness meets darkness—a border—but they cannot understand the shapes that borders demarcate. They cannot translate complex patterns of numbers into trees, houses, or other objects. In other words, they never really know what they are looking at.

Robots can only "see" when they are given specific information about what they are expected to see. For example, a robot that is first told how to recognize a road—say, by looking for two parallel borders—might be able to find a road in a simple scene that contained a straight (not curved) road in a particular orientation. But without advance knowledge about exactly what to look for in a particular scene, a robot is far more helpless when asked, "What do you see?" than a human infant would be.[5]

GROPING IN THE DARK

Instead of seeing what's around them, robots sense things in more primitive ways. Although some use cameras for limited purposes, most use sensors that provide simpler kinds of information than photographs do. The simplest sensors give the robot no sense of space at all, but merely reveal whether something is there or not. For example, sensors of *infrared energy* (red light humans can't see) can tell a robot whether it is very close to an object—and so might hit it—and *bump panels* can tell a robot when it does run into something.

More sophisticated sensors provide robots with vague clues about the structure of the space around them. For example, *laser range finders*, which emit an invisible beam of light that reflects off matter, can directly measure the distances and heights of nearby objects. Such a sensor is like a virtual whisker that contacts objects repeatedly with its tip to outline their contours.[6] The result might be a "view" made up of lines, short and tall, that jet up from the ground like stalagmites in a cave.

Sonar is another type of sensor. It employs the energy of sound waves. Like light, sound waves reflect off objects to reveal distance and shape information. Sonar can give machines a broad feel for the shape of surrounding objects—much like a person might get from using a hand to feel around a darkened room.[7] With sonar, a robot might see a scene of squared off bumps and valleys and floating shapes. But it wouldn't necessarily know what the pattern meant.

HALLUCINATING TRASH

Because robot sensory systems are poor, most mobile robots don't do a very good job of figuring out what's around them. For example, a robot named Egor in the Mobile Robotics Competition kept "hallucinating" trash because patches of light reflecting off the floor looked, to it, like wads of paper.[8] So Egor would roll over and try to "pick up" the light patches, which looked to the audience like empty space.

To avoid such mistakes, a robot can be tailored to fit a particular setting, accounting for such details as the color of walls, the lighting, and the texture of floors. However, that solution does not work in a real-world setting. The real world is too complex to describe to a robot in nauseating detail. Furthermore, it changes all the time. A programmer cannot anticipate every situation a robot might confront in a chaotic place.

GETTING AROUND—NOT

The biggest problem in building robots that can function in the real world, says computer scientist Reid Simmons of Carnegie-Mellon University, is that there is always a chance that something will "go wrong." What could go wrong? Consider the following scenarios.

* A floor is wet. A robot's wheels slip, and it slides across the floor—ending up someplace it hadn't planned to be. The robot continues moving in the direction specified in its plan as if nothing had happened and ends up careening down a flight of stairs.

* A robot is supposed to deliver a paper to room 212. When it arrives, the door is shut. The robot stops at the door and spins its wheels. It has no idea what to do.[9]

* A robot runs into a group of people huddled in a hallway. Its sensors detect a barrier, so the robot

A robot attempts to deliver a newspaper—a task it can do only under controlled circumstances.

thinks the hallway has ended. The robot decides to turn (as it was instructed to do at the real end of a hallway) and it runs into a wall.[10]

Things "go wrong" all the time in the real world. As people, we don't typically notice, since we adapt easily to most changes. We have common sense. For example, a person might knock on, or open, the door to room 212. No big deal. But traditional robots can't adapt. As a consequence, they end up doing stupid things whenever they're put in a complex, change-able setting, such as a messy office. People can try to "help" a robot by altering the environment for it—say, by replacing paper cups with towering boxes, which are easier for a robot to see. But doing so makes the setting far less realistic.

Most traditional robots also have very poor motor skills. In other words, they are clumsy. They lack the coordination to pick up small objects or to traverse bumpy, obstacle-strewn landscapes. Many mobile robots are extremely physically handicapped; they have neither arms nor legs.

Animal Smarts

For some or all of those reasons, various robot scientists decided, during the 1980s, to pave their own paths toward artificial intelligence. They abandoned the goal of mimicking human reasoning and decided to copy some of the survival skills possessed by simpler animals.

Animals have lots of skills that robot engineers wish robots had. Animals are fast, agile, and *adapt* well to their environments. Even cockroaches live remarkably well on their own in an ever-changing world. They can follow chemical trails, crawl around obstacles, pick up tasty morsels, and return to home base. A roach will show up any robot on an uncharted and ever-changing obstacle course.

So robot engineers began borrowing from biology, using animals as models for robots. Some robot engineers study animal movement, hoping to build robots with the agility to cross treacherous landscapes and obstacle-strewn rooms. Others try to mimic the reactive skills animals use to adapt to their habitats. Either way, they hope that copying nature's solutions will breed robotic wildlife that can take care of themselves, whether on snow-capped peaks or in hallways teeming with teenagers.

CHAPTER 4

ELECTRONIC ATHLETES: CATCHING UP WITH NATURE

A horse gallops gracefully through the forest, surefooted over knotty ground. A herd of pronghorn antelopes run across the open plains as fast as some cars motoring down a nearby highway. A cockroach hurries away from an approaching shoe, racing at blurring speed toward a crack in a wall.

Horses, pronghorns, and even cockroaches are remarkable athletes. While pronghorns can run fast enough to keep up with cars, many slower creatures move through a variety of natural obstacle courses with unthinking ease. Animals, from squirrels to centipedes, traverse forest, swamp, marsh, and jungle. They wade through mud, tromp over hills, weave in and out of bushes, squeeze into burrows, stomp over leaves, and even scurry up trees.

WALK AND ROLL

The physical skills of animals are remarkable when compared to the athletic prowess of most robots.

Most robots don't walk; they roll, and that can be a handicap. Although wheels work fine on smooth, hard surfaces, they perform poorly on soft or bumpy ground. They can get stuck in the mud or in rocky terrain. Wheeled machines can't step or hop over bumps and obstacles. They can't climb stairs, ladders, or trees. Because most natural terrain is not smooth and flat, anything on wheels is essentially barred from exploring nearly half the territory on Earth.[1]

So for more than a century, engineers have thought about building machines with legs. Legged robots could choose the best footholds along their route.[2] They could climb rock faces by placing their feet in widely spaced crevices; ladders by standing on the ladder's rungs (and not the in-between spaces!); or stairs by stepping upward and forward just the right amount so that their feet land on each horizontal platform. In short, a truly agile legged machine could go places that no machine with wheels has gone before.

THE CHALLENGE OF LEGS

Building a legged machine is more difficult than building a wheeled one. Wheels move in a simple way: They turn. But legs perform a complex stepping motion in which the leg bends and straightens at several joints as it rises and falls. In addition, a machine with more than one leg must coordinate its legs so that they work to move the machine forward without knocking into each other. Furthermore, the legs must support the robot's body, even as they step up and down, so that the robot maintains its balance.

One of the first mechanical stepping machines was built in 1870. The stepper had a series of cranks and levers that moved a body forward while the feet moved up and down in an alternating fashion.[3] The motion of the legs was determined by the way the parts of the stepper were linked together. (Such a stepping machine is called a *linkage*.) Like the automatons built 100 years earlier, the stepper's motion was always the same and could only be changed by taking the machine apart and then putting it back together in another way.

But a walking machine that cannot adjust its motions to fit its present environment is not very useful.[4] Useful walking machines must be able to adapt the way they walk to the task, terrain, and situation. In other words, they need some sort of brain. That brain could be a human, a computer, or both.

THE WALKING TRUCK

The first legged machine with a brain was the GE Walking Truck, a four-legged machine built in the mid-1960s by Ralph Mosher at General Electric. A person used his hands and feet to push the four pedals connected to the 3,000-pound (1,400-kg) machine's legs. The truck was part of a project to design advanced remote-controlled devices.

It was operated entirely by its human rider, who decided exactly how the truck would move. The machine could walk as fast as 4 miles per hour (2 m/s), the pace of a brisk human walk. It could also climb stacks of railroad ties and push jeeps out of the mud.[5]

SIX-LEGGED CRAWLERS

Four legs seems logical when a machine is controlled by human limbs. However, when the first walkers were built with limited computer "brains," scientists decided on six legs, the least number that

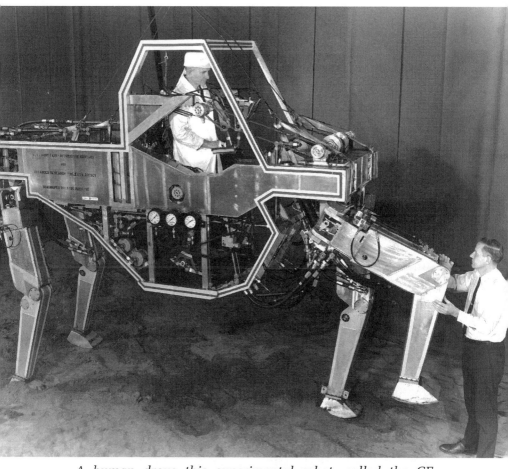

A human drove this experimental robot, called the GE Walking Truck, by pushing pedals that controlled the machine's legs.

could provide good stability during all phases of walking. Even with three legs off the ground, the robot would still be held up, like a stool, by a sturdy tripod of legs.[6]

Furthermore, in 1966, biologist Donald Wilson

had shown that insects commonly crawl using a tripod *gait*, or sequence of leg motions. That is, the animals walk by alternating between sets of three legs. Each set includes a front and a back leg on one side of the body and the middle leg on the other side of the body. And insects, which have been capably creeping over the planet for millions of years, seemed like good examples for robots to follow.[7]

So the first six-legged walking machines used a tripod gait. However, these slow, hulking machines were much less agile than insects are.

The First Hexapod
The first six-legged walker with a computer brain appeared at Ohio State University in 1977. The 300-pound (140-kg) machine could walk forward, turn, walk sideways, and crawl over simple obstacles. A computer made sure the hexapod remained level while walking over bumpy terrain by using information from sensors that detected tipping forces. The machine was stable only if it moved very slowly, at a speed of a few meters per minute.[8]

Hexapods of the 1980s
In the 1980s, three more six-legged machines appeared. One was built by Ivan Sutherland of Carnegie-Mellon University; another, called Odex-I, came from Odetics Inc. of Anaheim, California; and the third, called Adaptive Suspension Vehicle (ASV), emerged from the lab of Robert McGee and Kenneth Waldron at Ohio State University. All three machines were driven by people, who steered and controlled their speed while computers coordinated the stepping motions of the legs.

Each machine had a claim to stepping fame. For example, Odex once climbed into the back of a

This six-legged metallic "bug," called Odex-I, was not only stable, but also agile. It once climbed into the back of a pickup truck.

pickup truck and the 7,000-pound (3,200-kg) ASV trudged over railroad ties. But all were big and slow, with a top speed of about 3 feet per second (1 m/s).

Ambler
In the early 1990s, scientists at Carnegie-Mellon University in Pittsburgh built a 5,500-pound (2,500-kg),

six-legged machine called Ambler. Through a radio link, a human would steer Ambler in the right general direction while the robot used maps of the terrain to find the best footholds and paths around obstacles.

In early 1993, Ambler walked half a kilometer by itself—farther than any other legged robot had. But the machine was VERY slow, ambling at a speed of 3 feet per minute (1 m/min). Worse, it was unstable—a bad omen for a 2-ton beast.[9]

INCHING ON EIGHT LEGS

After Ambler, Carnegie-Mellon scientists decided to create an eight-legged robot. Their metallic spider, named Dante II, marched deep into the crater of a volcano in Alaska during the summer of 1994. Dante was controlled in the same way as Ambler, but it walked differently. Dante's legs were arranged like the legs of two tables, one inside the other. It walked by lifting one table of legs at a time, leaving the other "table" on the ground for support.[10]

Inching along in that way, Dante could travel forward, backwards, or sideways like a crab over steep, rocky, and even snowy terrain—but at a snail's pace of 3 feet per minute (1 m/min). Dante was not extremely agile either. It slipped and fell on its way out of the crater and broke one of its legs. The robot couldn't get up and had to be rescued by helicopter from its perch on a steep mountain slope.[11]

NOT LIKE THE ANIMALS

Those traditional six- or eight-legged robots may have looked like giant insects or spiders, but they didn't move much like insects or any other animal. Animals can walk quickly and run as well as leap, hop, and squeeze into holes. By comparison, all those walking robots were extremely slow, inflexible, and limited in their movements.

In addition, animal bodies bounce or swing up and down as they travel. The six-legged robots moved at an even pace and with as little jostling as possible. There was a time when engineers thought that such level movement would conserve energy and protect a robot's parts from damage. However, studies of walking and running animals by several biologists have suggested that the jostling motion may be better.

THE SECRET OF SPEED

Why are many-legged robots so slow? The major reason is the way they balance. Legged robots generally rely on *static stability*, a method used to balance stationary objects, such as stools. Static stability means that at every moment, even in the middle of a step, a robot must be completely balanced. Thus, at least three legs must be on the ground at all times.

In addition, a robot's *center of mass*, the point around which its bodyweight is equally distributed, must remain centered above the feet on the ground. For a six- or eight-legged robot, those criteria are not hard to satisfy, but they severely restrict movement.

That is why most animals—even six- or eight-legged ones—stay balanced on average over a step or a couple of steps, but not at every moment in time. For brief moments, moving animals often teeter on single legs or pairs of legs on one side of their bodies. There are many moments when a moving animal is unstable: If it were suddenly stopped, it would tip over.[12] If you don't believe it, try to stop walking right when one foot is about to hit the ground, when it's, say, 1 inch (2 cm) off the floor. You can't do it. You'll fall.

How do animals balance on average if they are unstable at many moments in time? If an animal is off balance in one direction, it will later compensate by becoming off balance in the opposite direction. An animal constantly makes these little corrections as it walks and runs. The corrections balance the animal over time. That is the principle of *active balance*.[13]

To better understand active balance, find a long, lightweight object, such as a broom or a poster tube. Rest the end of the broom's handle or either end of the tube on the palm of your hand. If you keep your hand still, the broom or tube will fall. Now move your hand back and forth to keep the object upright. Notice that to successfully do this, you must move your hand so that for every tipping of the broom or tube in one direction there is an equal tipping motion in the opposite direction. If you succeed, you are balancing the object actively.

Active balance is not only the secret of speed, but also the secret of flexibility. If an animal or robot can tolerate moments where it is slightly unbalanced, it can move its legs inward to squeeze through narrow openings, stretch a leg outwards to reach a distant foothold, jump over obstacles, or leap as it runs to increase speed.[14]

SAVING ENERGY

While animals gain speed and flexibility by balancing actively, they save energy by moving up and down as they walk and run. In the 1960s and 1970s, two Italian researchers thought up new ways of describing animal walking and running.[15] They said animals' bodies swing up and down while they walk, like pendulums, and bounce up and down while they run, like rubber balls or pogosticks. Whether walking or running, mammals' bodies *accelerate* (speed up) and *decelerate* (slow down) with each step. Unlike wheeled vehicles and most legged robots, walking and running animals move neither on a level plane nor at a constant speed.

Why do animals stop, start, and bounce when they move? It seems like a waste of energy. However, scientists have found that it is just the opposite. Animals' ways of walking and running actually conserve energy. To understand how, you'll need to better understand how pendulums and pogo sticks work.

A Swing in Their Steps

A *pendulum* is any object that hangs from a fixed point, usually on a rope or a chain, and swings freely under the force of gravity. A swing is a pendulum, and so is the long, vertical rod on a grandfather clock. A pendulum slows down and rises as it swings to one side and speeds up and falls as it moves toward the center of its range of motion.

A walking mammal moves like an upside-down pendulum. The torso is a weighted object that vaults up and down over the animal's legs, which act like a stiff rope or chain. The torso rises and slows down as the animal places its weight on a leg. Then the torso drops down and forward, gaining speed as the animal transfers its weight to the other foot.[16]

Walking in this way enables an animal to recycle some of the energy its muscles and tendons supply for walking. It does this by exchanging one form of energy for another.

When the animal's body rises, it gains gravitational *potential energy*, a form of energy associated with altitude. Then as the animal's body falls and moves forward, that potential energy is converted into *kinetic energy*, the energy of motion.[17] The kinetic energy is then converted back to potential energy in the next step. (A pendulum likewise interchanges potential energy and kinetic energy as it swings from its highest point to the center of its path and then up again on the other side.) By vaulting over somewhat stiffened legs, humans conserve up to 70 percent of the energy they put into walking.[18]

Pogo-Stick Prance

Animals conserve energy while running by using their legs as springs to bounce their bodies up and down. Biologists have learned that mammals have elastic structures in their legs that work as springs. As the animal's body springs upward, it speeds up, gaining both kinetic and potential energy at once. When the animal lands, it stores some of its energy in its legs as *elastic strain energy*, the kind of energy stored in a compressed spring.[19]

Elastic structures in the legs called *tendons*, which connect muscles to bones, stretch during each collision with the ground. The stored energy is released during the next step as the stretchy structures contract. For example, British zoologist R. McNeil Alexander of the University of Leeds has shown that kangaroos recycle energy from one step to the next by temporarily storing it in their Achilles tendons, large tendons that sit just above the heel of each foot. With a bouncing gait, some mammals can recycle as much as 40 percent of the energy their leg muscles supply while running.

A Lesson for Robots?

Principles such as active balance and energy storage in tendons are the secrets of nature that give animals a leg up on robots in athletics. Robots that could balance actively would be faster and more mobile than almost all of today's legged robots are.

They would also save precious energy. Energy efficiency seems to have been important in the evolution of animals and will be important in the design of legged robots when they are used commercially. In fact, the wasted heat energy generated by the six-legged robot called ASV was one reason the robot never had a full-time job.

Many biologists are trying to frame their findings in a language that robot engineers can use. We'll see an example of one such biologist in Chapter 6. But first you'll learn about Marc Raibert, a robot scientist who has used animal research to make robots run, leap, and perform other athletic feats.

CHAPTER 5

RAIBERT'S RUNNING ROBOTS

Clip, clop, B-O-I-N-G, clip, clop. The dome-shaped frame adorned with electronics runs on two springy legs across the hard floor of the lab. Then it jumps, flips its metallic body in the air, and lands on its feet to run some more.

A four-legged robot bounds down a hall. Clankity, clank, clank goes the headless metal horse as its creators run to catch up. Uh oh—a wall is approaching. A laboratory ranch hand quickly wrangles the horse before it collides with the wall.

A two-legged robot tries to flip, but doesn't rotate fast enough and takes a nose dive. Crash! Robot parts are everywhere. "Sometimes," says robot engineer Marc Raibert, "our laboratory doubles as a robot hospital."

Athletes do fall and get injured, and these are robot athletes. The world's only robot sprinters and gymnasts train in Raibert's cavernous basement lab—which Raibert calls the "Leg Lab"—at the Massachusetts Institute of Technology (MIT). For more than 15 years, Raibert and his coworkers have created a variety of fast, legged robots that run and balance on their own. Raibert hopes his research will yield a new breed of agile robots that can do things that no robot has done before.

LESSONS FROM A KITTEN

Raibert's robots are fast and agile in large part because they are modeled after animals. In fact, Raibert became interested in making running robots because he wanted to solve the secret of balance in animals.

Raibert first began to ponder the problem of balance while watching a film of a kitten walking on a treadmill in graduate school. Scientists had severed the links between the cat's brain and its body; yet, its legs continued to step almost normally. The film was supposed to show how normal walking could be without direction from the brain. But Raibert took home a different message.[1]

Raibert noticed that the "walking" cat had to be held up by its tail. Without intact connections to its brain, the cat could neither support nor balance its body. So Raibert wondered: How does an animal balance when it walks? What "rules" inside an animal's brain make it move its legs in a way that keeps its body upright?[2]

At about the same time, Raibert went to a conference on animal locomotion and heard a talk about a six-legged robot by an engineer named Robert McGee from Ohio State University. The audience laughed with surprise and delight as they watched a video of the oversized metallic ant that McGee and his colleagues had built (the 1977 hexapod). Raibert reacted more soberly. He thought: "That thing doesn't move like animals move," and decided to build a robot that did.[3]

Borrowing from Biology

So from the birth of the Leg Lab in 1980, Raibert had two goals in mind: agile robots and clues to the secret of animal balance. To learn to build robots that move like animals move, Raibert combed the biological literature for studies of animal motion.

Raibert latched onto two ideas from the studies he encountered. One was the fact that mammals have springy legs, which they use to hop like pogo sticks when they run. The other was active balance, the idea that running animals support their bodies differently than standing animals do. Unlike the six-legged robots, fast-moving animals don't keep a base of support beneath them at all times. Instead, they stay balanced on average over a step or two. (For more on active balance, see Chapter 4.)

Pogo-Stick Robot

But building a bouncing robot that balances actively is easier said than done. One big question was: How should the robot's "brain" coordinate its legs? The number of possible gaits (stepping patterns) for a creature with four or more legs is astronomical. McGee of Ohio State had found a mathematical formula for that number. The formula is $[(2k - 1)!]$ where "k" is the number of legs a creature has and "!" means "factorial."[4] According to that formula, a four-legged walker has more than 5,000 possible gaits, while a six-legged creature has almost 40 million possible gaits.

To simplify the problem, Raibert decided to build a one-legged machine, which by McGee's formula has one possible gait: It hops. The robot was modeled after a kangaroo, which can leap along in a gait called a "ricochet." That doesn't mean the robot looked like a kangaroo. It looked more like a dome

It doesn't look much like a kangaroo, but this one-legged hopper moved like one. In fact, the robot had to hop to stay upright.

on stilts, or rather, on a stilt. Later, Raibert built a robot that looked much more like a marsupial. It had a tail, which it used for balance, and an ankle joint that linked the leg to a foot.

But the first one-legged hopper only had a "hip," a hinge between its body and its leg. An umbilical cord connected the robot to a computer and several sources of power.[5]

To hop forward while keeping its balance, the robot's brain, which directs its motion, had to cooperate with its body, whose parts are configured to move in a certain way. Brain-body cooperation occurs in all animals. The computer issued commands based on information from the robot's sensors. The sensors measured things such as the angle between the body and the hip, and the length of the leg, then sent their measurements to the computer through the robot's umbilical cord.[6]

BOUNCING AND BALANCING

The robot's brain and body worked together to make the robot do three things: bounce, balance, and stand up straight. To make the robot bounce, Raibert gave the robot a springy leg like a mammal's. The spring in the leg was a cylinder of compressed air that expanded to make the robot spring upward and recompressed when the robot landed. The robot's computer brain controlled the height of each hop so that all hops were the same height. Like an animal's leg, the robot's springy leg stored energy. When the desired hopping height was achieved, most of the energy used for one hop was recycled for use in the next.

The computer kept the robot balanced as it hopped by placing the robot's foot in a particular place upon landing. The robot's foot position determined how much, and in which direction, the robot tilted. By controlling foot position, the computer made sure a tilt in one direction was balanced by equal tilt in the opposite direction. For example, the robot started running by leaning in the direction of its run. Then, in the air, the robot's leg swung forward so that it landed leaning in the opposite direction.

The robo-pogo kept its body upright by twisting a little at its hip every time it hit the ground. When the robot first landed, its body tipped backwards. So the computer directed hip motors to tilt the body forward relative to its leg.

With such control, the robot wouldn't even fall when a person pushed it. When a human used a joystick to control the robot's speed and direction, it reached a top speed of 4.8 miles per hour (2.2 m/s). The robot could hop in place, run along simple paths, and leap over objects.[7]

Two-Legged Track Star

A one-legged robot takes active balance to the "ultimate craziness," says biologist Robert Full: It can run but cannot stand still on its own. In this respect, Raibert's pogo-stick robot is about as different as possible from the slow six-legged robots others have built. That is exactly what Raibert had in mind. Raibert built his one-legged robot to prove that a robot could be made that bounced and balanced actively like animals do.

The next step was to add more legs.

In 1986, Raibert and coworkers Jessica Hodgins and Jeff Koechling made a two-legged version of the pogo-stick robot that runs along a circle on the floor. Like the one-legged robot, the aluminum *biped* has springy legs. Like a human, the biped runs with an alternating gait: It lands and pushes off with its left leg on one step and does the same with its right leg on the next step. At any one time, only one of the robot's legs is active. So the scientists used the con-

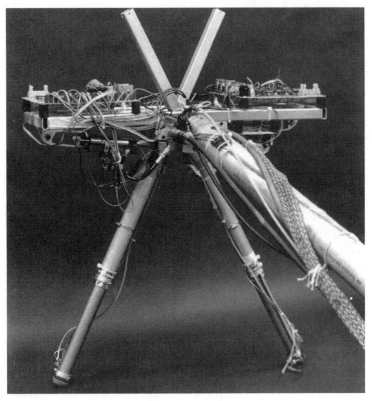

This two-legged contraption is the fastest legged robot in the world. It can also do flips.

trols from the one-legged robot for the active leg of the biped.[8]

The running biped set the world speed record for legged robots: 13 miles per hour (6 m/s). That is about the average speed of the fastest human marathon runners, but still much slower than an ostrich, which can run up to 50 miles per hour (22 m/s). The robot can hop on one leg or switch back and forth between one-legged hopping and regular running. The biped has also climbed stairs made of wooden blocks, jumped over blocks, and flipped in the air.[9]

Rᴏʙᴏ-Gʏᴍɴᴀꜱᴛꜱ

The 1986 biped is not only the fastest robot in the world, but also the first running robot gymnast. Its main trick is the forward flip. When the robot flips, the computer commands it to do just what coaches tell human gymnasts: Jump high and tuck tight. A "hurdle step" prepares the robot to flip by generating extra hopping height, which gives the robot more time to rotate.[10]

The robot tucks its legs during the "flip step" to make its body spin faster. A body's rate of spin increases when the mass of that body is concentrated near its center of mass, the point around which the body's weight is equally distributed. An ice skater uses the same principle to twirl faster by bringing the arms and legs in closer to the body.[11]

Upon landing, the robot's springy legs absorb some of its energy by using it to help power the next running step. The computer also returns the robot to its normal running posture by exerting twisting forces (*torques*) on the robot that cancel out the spinning energy left over from the flip.[12]

The robo-gymnast also can perform aerials (no-handed cartwheels). However, the robot is not as good at doing aerials as it is at doing flips. Aerials require pushing off with one leg instead of two, and that technique often doesn't enable the robot to get high enough to rotate its body all the way around before hitting the ground.[13]

The first robo-gymnast pranced, leaped, and flipped from the end of a pole called a boom. Its descendant, built 3 years later, runs and flips on its own. It stands on an elevated treadmill in the lab, connected to a bunch of ropes called a "wrangling harness." The robot uses the harness to practice its flips, just as a gymnast uses spotting ropes to practice tricks on a trampoline.

Gɪᴅᴅʏ-ᴜᴘ Rᴏʙᴏᴛ

After building his first biped, Raibert set out to apply what he'd learned to a four-legged robot. Coordinating four legs presents the following problem: Balance is better when the legs swing under a body's center of mass, which is right where the legs are likely to crash into each other. However, Raibert found a way to get around that problem. He programmed the computer to treat pairs of legs positioned far from each other as single "virtual legs" located at the center of the body. In that way, a four-legged machine becomes a machine with two virtual legs, which can be programmed to move in the same way as a two-legged robot.[14]

For a four-legged robot or animal, there are three possible sets of leg pairs: diagonal pairs, right and left pairs, or front and back pairs. These pairs are capable of three simple gaits that many four-legged animals use. With the legs paired diagonally, the robot prances along in a *trot*. When its legs are paired sideways, the robot speeds along in pace. And when its front legs act as a pair and its back legs as the other pair, the robot *bounds*.[15]

All three gaits rely on active balance. When the robot paces, it tilts from side to side as its right and left leg pairs alternately support the body. Similarly, when the robot bounds, it pitches forward and backward. The robot stays balanced because the swaying is symmetrical. A tilt in one direction is matched by a tilt in the opposite direction. Animals do the same thing when they trot and bound.

Raibert's headless metallic horse can trot, pace, and bound. It balances by matching a tilt in one direction with a tilt in the opposite direction.

Raibert's four-legged creature is fast for a robot, but slow compared to animals. It runs fastest when bounding, and its maximum speed is only about 6 miles per hour (3 m/s).

LUNAR POGOS AND RESCUE ROBOTS?

Most of the robots Raibert has built over the years have "retired" from athletics. They hang like huge metallic mobiles from the ceiling of Raibert's Leg Lab. Only the most recent two-legged gymnast still stands in its harness, poised to practice its tricks.

Nevertheless, the lessons learned from Raibert's running robots will undoubtedly enable robots to go places that no robot can go today. With legs, robots might explore new territories from Mars to remote regions of Earth such as Antarctica, the jungles of Surinam, and the Australian outback. Possibly such robots could recover valuable mineral deposits or other treasures in these lands.

In the early 1970s, various people proposed building legged rovers to explore the moon, which at the time was believed to be carpeted with soft dust that a wheeled vehicle could not traverse.[16] In 1967, a Stanford University professor named H. Seifert even suggested that a giant pogo-stick robot, which he called a "Lunar Pogo," might be an efficient way of traveling on the moon, where low gravity would enable very long hops.[17]

Legged robots might replace humans in dangerous jobs on Earth such as exploring volcanoes, fighting fires, working in nuclear power plants, and diving into the ocean. Very agile robots might even hike up mountains to rescue freezing, exhausted, or injured climbers.

Legged robots might also help the military by carrying wounded soldiers or transporting troops across rough country. In the 1940s, British engineers proposed building a 1,000-ton walking tank, and 20 years later, the army planned to use a four-legged "truck" to transport troops ashore from ships.[18] In 1945, inventor Henry Wallace patented a one-legged hopping tank that was supposed to be hard to hit because of its odd, unpredictable way of moving.[19] At the time, no one could implement the idea. Now, of course, someone could.

LEGS WITHOUT A BRAIN

But Raibert says he'll leave the moonbots to someone else. Now he's aiming to break his old speed records. He wants to test the limits of robot speed on legs. He says there's room for improvement, since his robots weren't really built with speed in mind. Raibert is also testing how much of a legged robot's motion can be built into the mechanical structure itself without sensors or even a computer brain.

"We're interested in structures designed so that they can do mechanical maneuvers on their own," Raibert says. Already, he's watched colleagues build a pair of metallic legs with no electronic parts that can strut upright across a surface by themselves!

Raibert admits he faces a tough challenge. It's hard to beat animal parts when it comes to mechanical prowess. Not even steel and the bulletproof kevlar, he says, can stand up to bone.

CHAPTER 6

CREEPY SECRETS FROM NATURE

A cockroach dashes down a tiny track in a laboratory at the University of California at Berkeley. The insect's leg muscles contract forcefully, propelling the thumb-sized body at lightning speed over the platform. Biologist Robert Full watches this animal as a jockey might admire a horse. Although Full knows he had nothing to do with the insect's athletic prowess, he's delighted to have discovered its talent.

Before Full took an interest in cockroaches, biologists had only watched insects crawl and scurry; nobody had carefully measured their movements. So many scientists were surprised when Full discovered just how graceful and fast some insects can be. On the wall of Full's office hangs a framed clipping from the *1993 Guinness Book of World Records*. It announces the world record for the fastest running insect—set by a cockroach in Full's lab.

The record-setting insect, an American cockroach, was clocked at about 3.4 miles per hour (about 1.5 m/s). It covered a distance equal to fifty of its body lengths per second. "These are the sprinters,"

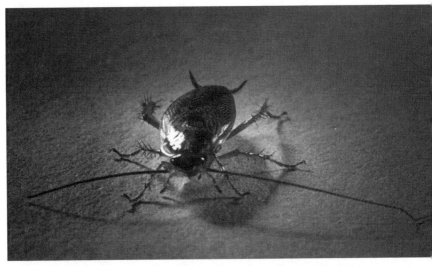

A product of 350 million years of evolution, the cockroach is built for both balance and speed.

says Full, "the ones you think you don't have in your kitchen."

Roaches are not the only crawling creature whose image has been given a lift by Full's research. Crabs, once thought to be slow and clumsy, have turned out to be very good runners—yes, runners—according to Full.

Full's research also reveals why crabs and cockroaches are so fast and agile. It turns out that these critters do not, as researchers had assumed, move like today's statically stable-legged robots. Instead, they move surprisingly like horses, cheetahs, and other mammals. The principles of movement Full has uncovered from studying crabs and cockroaches have exciting implications for the design of legged robots. Engineers have already begun to use his findings to create more agile robotic creatures.

Universal Secrets

As a biologist, Full did not set out to study robots. Instead, he wanted to discover very general principles about how skeletons work to move bodies. At the time Full began his research, biologists had already gathered lots of information about how mammals move. But Full aspired to uncover truly universal secrets of nature. To do that, he needed to look for similarities between very different types of animals. Since the data on mammals existed, he decided to study animals that are as unlike mammals as possible.[1]

He chose cockroaches and crabs not because these animals are cute, but because they seem to have little in common with their more cuddly relatives. Roaches and crabs have more legs than mammals have, much smaller and more primitive brains than mammals do, and skeletons called *exoskeletons* that lie on the outside of the body instead of under the flesh, as mammals' skeletons do.

Full's choice of animal may also have been motivated by a lifelong fascination with many-legged critters. "When I was small, I liked weird animals," Full says. "Instead of a fish tank, I had a crab tank." As a boy, Full watched his crabs climb over rocks and wondered how they did that. As a scientist, he says, he can continue to explore the legged wonders that amazed him as a child. Only now he can find answers to the questions he could previously only ponder.

Miniature Runways

To find out how crabs and cockroaches move, Full does experiments in which he carefully observes the animals' body movements as they walk and run. This style of research, in which a scientist examines the physical forces exerted on living things, is known as *biomechanics.* Among other things, Full measures the forces on the animals' legs, their speeds, and their energy use.

To measure leg forces, Full and his coworkers lead cockroaches and crabs down runways and over fancy "scales" called *force plates.* A force plate not only measures the vertical force (weight) of a body, as an ordinary scale does, but also the forward and sideways forces produced by a body that runs across it. For cockroaches, the force plate is tiny and so sensitive that when a person blows on it, the plate registers the pressure from the puff of air. When the cockroach is done walking or running, the force plate data are sent to a computer for analysis.[2]

In some experiments with cockroaches, Full has the animals run over a slab of Jell-O™, which he discovered can function like a force plate to reveal the force acting on a single cockroach leg. When a cockroach's foot presses down on the Jell-O™, the Jell-O™ compresses, and a light underneath the Jell-O™ makes the compressed area light up. The splotch of light under the insect's foot can then be measured and used to determine the force on its leg: The bigger the splotch, the bigger the force.[3]

In addition to his force-plate measurements, Full films the animals with a high-speed video camera, which takes 1,000 pictures per second! Pictures from the camera are also fed into the computer. The computer analyzes the pictures to reveal an animal's leg and body movements, its speed, and how the animal's movements relate to the forces on its body.[4]

BUILT TO BOUNCE
From such studies, Full has found that cockroaches run with a springlike, bouncing gait similar to the

one mammals use when they run. Such findings not only bring to light similarities between very different beasts, but also overturn previous notions of cockroach movement. Scientists had thought that cockroaches travel without jostling, at an even speed—like a wheeled vehicle—and that they stay stable like a stool using a *tripod gait*: Three legs step at a time while the other three legs support the insect. Most six-legged robots were based on this model of insect walking.

Walking cockroaches do use a tripod gait when running slowly, says Full. However, the insects don't move like a wheel when they jog. Instead of running at a constant speed, cockroaches speed up and slow down with each step. And instead of staying level, roaches' bodies rise and fall as they run.

As a cockroach pushes off with one set of three legs, its body accelerates and springs upward. As the animal's body falls back down, it decelerates, and tissues in its legs bend. Its bent legs store energy like a bowed pole that's about to launch a pole vaulter upward. Like mammals, roaches conserve energy by storing it in their legs upon landing and releasing it on takeoff.

Racing Roaches

When cockroaches run really fast, says Full, they may even abandon the tripod gait. He found that, when moving at very high speeds, roaches don't always keep at least three legs on the ground. Instead, the animals often teeter on fewer legs, relying on active balance (see Chapter 4) to stay upright, just as running mammals do.

Racing cockroaches, for example, can run on just their two back legs. Full discovered that speeding roaches lift their bodies up and cock their heads upwards as if stretching for the finish line. (Similarly, fast-moving centipedes sometimes balance on just three of their forty-four legs!) At very high speeds, a running roach may soar into the air momentarily, lifting all six of its legs off the ground.[5] Ghost crabs, too, sometimes leap into the air as they scurry sideways on eight legs.[6, 7]

Thus, when moving fast, even many-legged creatures are not stable at every moment in time like a stool. If a speeding cockroach were suddenly stopped, it would probably flip or tip over. But while moving quickly, cockroaches, crabs, and even centipedes keep their balance by matching a body tilt in one direction with a tilt in the other.

Natural Inspiration

Thus, the lessons learned from creatures as different as crabs and cheetahs suggest that stool-like stability and wheel-like motion are fine for moving at slow speeds. However, those traits are not desirable for any legged creature, whether natural or robotic, that needs to move quickly. To move fast, robots with any number of legs should balance actively, Full says.

More importantly, Full's animal research proves that legged robots don't have to trade stability for speed. It is possible to have both. Lessons from many-legged animals show that robots with six or eight legs can combine excellent static stability with the ability to move quickly. While standing still or walking slowly, a robot could support itself solidly using several legs and a sprawled posture. But by employing active balance and a bouncing gait, such a robot could also move quickly while conserving energy.

A Cockroach Robot

Although no one wants to build a six-legged beast that invades cereal boxes, roboticists in several American laboratories are using Full's findings to create agile, electronic creepy-crawlies. Raibert is using them to create a realistic *computer simulation* of moving insects and crabs. A computer simulation is an experiment in which computerized creatures act in an electronic world under the influence of electronic "forces" similar to physical forces in the real world.

The crabs and cockroaches Raibert created (with help from Full and his coworkers) will combat electronic gravity and friction using simulated muscles in the creatures' legs. They will move at the same speeds and with the same accelerations and decelerations as their real-life counterparts. These computer-created animals can serve as moving blueprints for robots, and so promise to be useful to anyone who wants to build a six- or an eight-legged robot.

Michael Binnard, a graduate student in Rodney Brooks's lab at MIT, is doing just that. Binnard is using Full's research to construct a six-legged robot with legs like those of a real cockroach. Binnard's cockroach robot, which he calls Boadicea, will have front legs, middle legs, and hind legs that are different from one another—just as, Full has learned, the leg pairs in a cockroach are.

Each pair of the robot's legs will be structured like its cockroach counterpart and so suited to the kind of motion that counterpart performs. For example, the back legs will be structured in a way that makes them good for pushing off and accelerating the robot, and the front legs will be designed to effectively slow down or stop the robot.

Binnard's robot is almost done, and Full couldn't be more thrilled. The biologist never dreamed his research on crab and cockroach locomotion would contribute to such metallic creations. "You never know what will grow out of basic research," he says. "It's spectacular."

CHAPTER 7

BUGBOTS, MOONDOZERS, AND OTHER SIMPLEMINDED MACHINES

A rocket lands on the moon. A door opens and a small six-legged robot crawls out the door and onto the lunar surface. Seconds later, another robot emerges; a third follows. Soon dozens of electronic critters are swarming over the moon like a colony of oversized metallic ants.

Take Two: *A spaceship lands. Tiny bulldozers scoot down a ramp from the spaceship onto the lunar sand. The robots start digging trenches and tunnels to prepare the site for a future human colony. Every once in a while, they stop to sunbathe so that they can recharge their solar-powered batteries.*

Rodney Brooks, a robot scientist at the Massachusetts Institute of Technology (MIT), can picture such futuristic scenes in his mind. Brooks plays out his vision inside a glass-walled space in his laboratory called the "sandbox," a knobby landscape of rocks, hills, and holes. In the sandbox, three six-legged robots, several "moondozers" on tanklike tracks, and other small electronic critters practice their skills for rambling over rough ground like that on the moon and Mars.

The robots in the sandbox are some of the dozens of small, animal-like robots that Brooks and his coworkers in the Mobile Robot (Mobot) Lab have built over the past decade. Like an ant sniffing out a path to candy, or a waterbug shimmying across a field, Brooks's robots are not brilliant beasts. They never think about, or even know, what they are doing. Instead, like insects and other primitive animals, they instinctively avoid obstacles, step over holes, and perform other mindless maneuvers that enable them to survive in a chaotic universe.

BIG BRAINS, LITTLE MINDS

Fifteen years ago, small, simpleminded robots like those that populate the Mobot Lab were virtually unheard of. Back then, the field of artificial intelligence called for big, complex robots that reason like people do. Such robots had specific knowledge of a particular place in the world and the ability to think and plan out their actions. Such a strategy led to robots, like Shakey (see Chapter 3), that were slow and limited to simple settings made especially for them.

When Brooks entered the field of AI, he was not impressed with Shakey or any of its contemporaries. Brooks didn't believe in babying robots by giving them special places to be. Like wild animals, he reasoned, robots should be equipped to deal with changeable habitats. They should work while visitors or cleaners walk around them, when furniture is rearranged, when lights dim or brighten, and when their sensors give faulty readings.

As a graduate student at Stanford University in

Palo Alto, California, Brooks watched the brilliant roboticist Hans Moravec program a robot using traditional methods. Moravec's robot had a central brain with a goal: to get to the other end of a room that was littered with trash cans and desks. Its brain also contained knowledge of things in its environment and a map of the room. The robot used its map to figure out where it was at all times and where it should go next to move nearer to its goal.[1]

Moravec's robot turned out to be one of the smartest mobile robots the world had seen. But even this machine didn't impress Brooks. The robot was extremely slow. It would sit for 15 minutes thinking about its next move, move a meter, and then stop to think some more.[2] In short, the big-brained machine was nowhere near as bright as a bug.

BUILT TO BEHAVE

Brooks realized that insects with very simple brains are able to scurry around, speedily performing tasks that include collecting food and stinging enemies. Insects don't think carefully about what they are doing and yet they can do much more than Moravec's big-brained robot could. So Brooks thought: Why not build a robot with the brains of a bug?

To find a strategy for such a machine, Brooks began reading biology papers. He learned how animals, without maps or plans, have evolved simple behaviors that enable them to respond quickly to what's going on around them and so adapt to their environments. What Brooks learned about the natural world inspired him to invent a new design for robots.

The design for Brooks's so-called "behavior-based" robots calls for several small computer "brains" (processors) instead of one big, central brain. Each small processor governs a simple animal-like behavior that does not involve modeling or planning. Instead, each behavior links a robot's sensors directly to its motors so a robot can react quickly to its immediate situation. In essence, each processor triggers a speedy knee-jerk reaction—such as moving away from light or toward sound—when conditions are right.

The most basic of these reactions are those, such as "lift leg" and "avoid objects," that take care of details and keep the robot out of trouble. Higher-level behaviors satisfy less urgent goals such as "find door" and "track prey." Basic behaviors can operate while a goal is being pursued. This means that a robot can step over a hole *while* it is looking for a door. However, behaviors sometimes conflict and one processor *suppresses* (blocks the outputs of) another. For example, if a robot senses an obstacle ahead, its "avoid obstacle" brain suppresses forward motion and prompts motors to turn or back up.

ALLEN

In 1986, Brooks and his students built the first behavior-based robot. The cylindrical wheeled robot, named Allen, had three simple behaviors. The most basic was "avoid obstacles"; Allen would sit around without moving until a person approached it. Then it would roll away, using its sonar sensors to avoid collisions as it went.[3]

Allen's second behavior was "follow walls." As Allen did that, its "avoid obstacles" behavior kept it a safe distance from the wall. A third behavior, "find doors," caused Allen to scurry toward any gap in a wall while "avoid obstacles" kept it away from the doorjamb.[4]

With the various brains working together, Allen would scoot away from people, along walls, and through doors. From a bunch of simple actions, complex behavior emerged as if by magic. Allen had no goals in life. It didn't even know what it was doing, and yet the robot acted as if it *wanted* to move away from people and *planned* to roll through doors on its way somewhere. At times, Allen even seemed alive.

Snail on Wheels

After Allen, the Mobot Lab's next big project was Herbert, a robot designed to roll around offices and grab soda cans off desks. Built by graduate student Jon Connell, Herbert was a more complex robot than Allen; it had more sensors and more behaviors. It also had a gripper arm. And unlike Allen, which was tethered to a big computer, Herbert carried its computer brains with it (on board). Its brains were a group of circuit boards bound to its body like tiles on a bathroom wall. Each postcard-sized board governed one of Herbert's simple behaviors.[5]

Some of Herbert's behaviors were inspired by studies of specific animals. One such study, by biologist Niko Tinbergen, showed that baby gulls may confuse crude models of gull heads with the heads of their parents. The study suggested that baby gulls recognize Mom and Dad by the *shapes* of their heads and not by their facial features. Similarly, Herbert was programmed to recognize a soda can by an outline of its shape.[6]

The general structure of Herbert's brain was inspired by the coastal snail *Littorina*, an animal that is ruled by simple reflexes. The snail's reflexes include "up," which tells the snail to crawl against gravity, and "dark," which makes it crawl away from light. Herbert was given equally simple reflexes such as "lift arm" and "grasp."[7]

When linked together, Herbert's simple reflexes created complex behavior. If Herbert saw a soda-can-like thing, a reflex told its wheels to stop. That action would trigger its arm to rise. The rising of its arm would then, in turn, prompt a series of reflexes that would ultimately position Herbert's gripper around a soda can. At that point, Herbert would sense an object—it wouldn't know what—between the halves of its gripper, and it would grab.[8]

Herbert had no knowledge of the world or any concept of its mission. Yet when Herbert was working—which wasn't often since it was always knocking into things and breaking—its reflexes produced the illusion of purposeful behavior.[9]

After Herbert was retired in 1989, other wheeled robots were built. Then Brooks decided to create a robot that could walk.

A BEASTLY BUGBOT

The six-legged metallic bug lies still on the floor. Its legs, woven with wires and switches, are splayed out flat. Somebody flips a switch. As power flows into the creature's electronic innards, it comes to life. The body rises. Its heat-sensing "eyes" and metal whiskers start sensing its surroundings. "Thweep, thweep," the critter cries as it scuttles across the floor.[10]

In 1988, the Mobot Lab's first walking robot, Genghis, was born. Built by Colin Angle, then a college student, the 2-pound (1-kg) robot can stand up, walk over and around obstacles, and chase "prey" (moving bodies). Like its ancestors, Genghis is not controlled by one central brain. Instead, its behaviors emerge

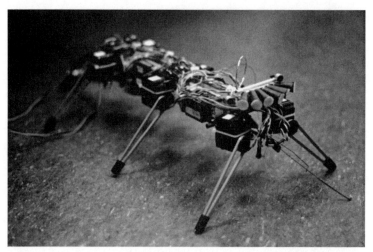

Behavior-based bug: Genghis, the Mobot Lab's first walking robot, would step over obstacles and chase people around a room.

from the collective workings of several simple "brains"—in this case, little software programs.

For normal walking, each of Genghis's legs has a behavior that says, "If I'm back, swing forward; if I'm forward, push back." So each leg goes through a cycle of motion on its own, generating the step cycle. That behavior was inspired by studies of walking insects. These studies suggest that the motions of insect legs are controlled by groups of cells in each leg and not by a part of the insect brain.

To coordinate its legs, Genghis has a behavior that makes its legs take turns swinging. Although insects probably don't have such a turn-taking mechanism, that behavior plus the individual leg behaviors enable the robot to walk with an insectlike ripple gait over flat ground.[11]

Genghis can also crawl over small objects by

using a "collide" behavior, which makes any leg that hits an obstacle lift higher so it clears the obstacle. In this way, Genghis can climb over books and other small obstacles better than most preprogrammed robots, which may stumble over objects unless they are told beforehand what and where the objects are. Genghis first "knows" about an object when its foot hits it.[12]

Genghis also has a high-level behavior that directs it toward prey. When the robot's *pyroelectric sensors*, which detect heat, sense a warm body that's moving, they activate this predatory behavior, causing the robot to "hunt down" people in the lab.[13]

Bug Brothers

After Genghis, two somewhat larger six-legged robots, Attila and Hannibal, cropped up in the Mobot

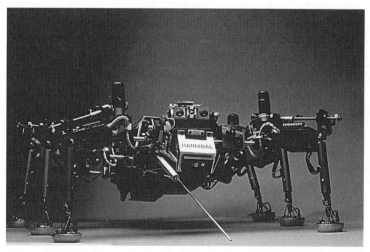

Hannibal, Genghis's big brother, can switch between three gaits like insects do, and it can sense holes before it steps into them.

Lab. Attila and Hannibal are almost twins. Hannibal, built by Colin Angle and programmed by graduate student Cynthia Ferrell, is the smarter and more agile of the two. "Hannibal is probably the most complex robot in the world for its size," says Ferrell. Compared to Genghis, Hannibal has more sensors, motors, joints, and computer power as well as more buglike behaviors.

In designing the software for Hannibal, Ferrell was inspired by a theory of cockroach locomotion developed by biologist Kier Pearson in the 1970s. Pearson proposed that the motions of each cockroach leg are controlled by cells in that leg. In addition, Pearson supposed that the walking cells in different legs communicate with each other to coordinate the insect's gait.[14]

With Pearson's ideas in mind, Ferrell linked the circuits that controlled Hannibal's legs so the legs could communicate with each other. The result was a robot that walks more like insects than Genghis does. For example, Hannibal switches between three gaits as it picks up its pace, as insects are known to do. Genghis, by contrast, has only one gait.[15]

For walking over uneven terrain, Ferrell drew from studies of locusts. For example, in the 1980s, biologists found that a locust will wave a leg up and down, searching for a foothold, whenever its leg can't find a supportive spot of ground. So, like a locust, Hannibal will perform "searching motions" whenever it's about to step in a hole or over a cliff.[16] Genghis cannot sense dips in the terrain and so tends to fall into holes and walk over cliffs.

Small Success

Robots like Genghis, Attila, and Hannibal could change the face of robotics. Such robots not only stomp down conventions about intelligence but also trample dogma about size. Most people envision large, or at least people-sized, robots doing things for humanity. For example, a robot the size of Mom or Dad is easy to imagine wandering around the house vacuuming, using its arms to move furniture out of the way. But Brooks has a better idea: A hoard of tiny dirt-eating robots could crawl under furniture and into tight spaces to slurp up grime.[17]

Outer space is another good habitat for small robots. In past years, the National Aeronautics and Space Administration (NASA) has sponsored projects to develop robots that could explore other planets. In 1990, NASA funded 5,500-pound (2,500-kg) Ambler (see Chapter 4) as well as Attila and Hannibal. "At that time," Ferrell says, "Ambler was our *big* competition."

Brooks sees Ambler-like machines as poor competition for small planetary rovers. Dozens or hundreds of shoe-sized robots, he says, could be sent into space for the price of one Ambler. In addition, small robots are less likely to be destroyed than a hulking machine. "Hannibal is 6 inches off the ground. If it falls—so what?" says Ferrell. Even if a small robot did get hurt, there would be other robots to carry out the mission. An additional advantage of sending lots of robots into space is the ability to direct different robots to do tasks at separate locations. One big robot could only do one thing at a time and, if it broke, all would be lost.[18]

CRAWLING COMPUTER CHIPS

But Hannibal and his predecessors are too big for Anita Flynn, an engineer in Brooks's lab. In 1988, Flynn and her coworkers built Squirt, a 1.25-cubic-inch (19.5-cm³) "spy bug" that scoots under chairs

Hardly bigger than a nickel, Squirt acts somewhat like a tiny robot spy, hiding in dark places and "listening" for noise. Future versions of Squirt may be as small as pennies.

and into other dark places, hiding until it hears a noise.[19] When the noise disappears, Squirt comes out of hiding, moving in the direction of the noise. It then hides again to listen for more "secrets."

Like the Mobot Lab's other robots, Squirt owes its behavior to an electronic pyramid of simple actions. The wheeled bug does not understand the idea of hiding. It simply moves away from light—the work of its lowest layer. Monitoring a light sensor, Squirt moves in a spiral pattern searching for darkness. Once safe in the shadows, Squirt stops and the second layer takes over. That layer listens for noises by monitoring two microphone "ears." When a noise is detected, the bug moves toward it. After the robot has traveled a certain distance, level one kicks in again and Squirt finds a new hiding place.

In its tiny body, the size of a big pencil eraser, Squirt holds a computer, power supply, sensors, and motors to make it go. But to Flynn, it is still too big. Flynn wants to make a computer chip get up and walk. She envisions cheap, throwaway robots the size of pennies or smaller that would have their motors, brains, sensors, and power supplies etched onto one piece of silicon. Flynn is now working on shrinking the size of the motors she needs to make tiny robots that she calls "gnats." At the same time, several of Flynn's students are crafting smaller versions of Squirt.

Ultimately, Flynn and her team plan to make robots small enough to crawl into the smallest crevices of the human body. Electrical engineering student James McLurkin has made a wheeled robot the size of a large marble that he hopes will lead to even smaller robots that can roll inside a human intestine to perform surgery from the inside. As miniature surgeons, future gnat robots also might creep into clogged arteries to clean them out, or sew delicate stitches in eyes.

Miniature mobile robots could have uses outside of medicine, too. They might trim lawns by nibbling the grass blade by blade. They might toil as tiny construction workers to align optical fibers or bond wires to chips. A swarm of gnat robots might live on your scalp and style your hair, strand by strand. Thousands of gnat robots could explore the moon or Mars, spread by the wind or hopping on silicon springs. The tiny rovers would send their findings to Earth, but would be "out of control," says Flynn, of anyone on Earth.[20]

ROBOTS WITH NERVE

The small, six-legged creature crawling on the computer screen is hungry, but it can't get to its food. A long wall, which it detects with one wiry antenna, stands between it and the delicious morsels it smells. What will it do? Will it try to crawl through the wall and be stopped? Will it just give up and look for food somewhere else?

Computer scientist Randall Beer, who created this electronic animal, is not even sure. He didn't program the insect with any knowledge of what to do in such situations. But Beer's suspense is relieved as the insect on the screen "chooses" to do what any right-minded real insect would. It follows the wall until it detects a break in the barrier. Then it goes through the opening and heads straight toward the food.

How did this insect, which lives in a computer-bound playground with virtual food, obstacles, and odors, get to be so smart? The insect has no brain.

But it does have a brainlike structure that was inspired by animal *nervous systems*—weblike networks of cells that control much of animals' behavior.

Like Brooks and his coworkers, Beer and his research team at Case Western Reserve University in Cleveland, Ohio, are creating artificial creatures and robots that have the smarts used by primitive animals to survive in the world. But unlike Brooks, Beer sticks very close to biology. Instead of just reproducing animal behavior, Beer mimics the biological structures that underlie that behavior.

Beer hopes that by copying nature's solutions as precisely as possible, he will create robots that are as independent and capable as animals are. So far, Beer and his team have built two six-legged robots that are modeled closely after animals or parts of animals. Beer hopes to someday build a robot that is capable enough to wander the real world, doing simpleminded chores such as picking up trash, mowing a lawn, and mopping a floor.

THE COMPUTER COCKROACH

In 1988, Beer made his first attempt at mimicking nature with electronics. Then a graduate student in computer science, Beer and Hillel Chiel, a Case Western biologist, set out to create the artificial insect. They named the insect *Periplaneta computatrix* after the natural creature that inspired it— *Periplaneta americana*, the American cockroach.[1]

To create *P. computatrix*, Beer and Chiel first drew it on the computer. They made a head, a mouth, two antennae, six legs with feet, and a five-sided body. Then they added sensors—taste buds on the mouth, smell and pressure sensors on the antennae, and leg-position sensors to detect when a leg was all the way forward or all the way back. They also gave the insect a sensor in its gut that gauges "hunger," a sign that the insect's electronic energy store is running low.[2]

In addition, the scientists gave *P. computatrix* imaginary "muscles," which move its legs and mouth. Its legs can move up and down, back and forth, and side to side. Its mouth can open and close.[3]

With sensors and muscles, the insect could sense its environment and it could move. But to act appropriately in various situations, it needed a system that tied sensations of the environment to movements.

Who's Got Nerve?

In an animal nervous system, special cells called *nerve cells* or *neurons* link sensations and actions by sending chemical messages from sensory receptors in the eyes, ears, and other sensory organs to nerve cells, and ultimately, to muscles.

Nerve cells are connected to one another in web-like networks that control behaviors. The networks are set up so that, most of the time, only the behaviors most appropriate to the current situation are active. In that way, its nervous system enables an animal to adapt to its environment.

To help *P. computatrix* adapt to its electronic world, Beer and Chiel gave it an artificial nervous system. With just 78 computer-coded neurons, that artificial nervous system is very simple compared to most animal nervous systems: Even insect nervous systems typically contain hundreds of thousands of neurons.[4] Nevertheless, this simplified system generated five insectlike behaviors: walking, wandering, wall following, food finding, and eating.

In *P. computatrix*, each behavior is controlled by

a separate circuit of electronic neurons. Two of those circuits—the ones for walking and feeding—were inspired by what biologists know about specific neural circuits in animals.

Wɐʟᴋ Lɪᴋᴇ ɐ ᴃᴜɢ

The circuit that controls walking in *P. computatrix*, like the one in Hannibal, is based on biologist Kier Pearson's model of cockroach locomotion. However, this circuit follows Pearson's model in a more detailed way than the circuit in Hannibal does.

Pearson's model not only suggests that each cockroach leg is controlled independently, but also specifies a network of nerve cells in each leg. The networks include sensory neurons that sense a leg's position and the weight it supports, and also motor neurons, which trigger movement.

In addition, according to Pearson's model, each leg network has a "rhythm generator," a neuron that turns "on" and "off" (becomes active and then inactive) at regular intervals. When a leg's rhythm generator is on, the leg swings forward. When it is off, the leg stays anchored to the ground, pushing back and moving the body forward. And so each leg swings to the beat of its own nerve-cell "drummer."

Inspired by Pearson's model, Beer gave each leg of *P. computatrix* a group of electronic nerve cells. Each group had three motor neurons, two sensory neurons, and one "pacemaker" neuron (the rhythm generator). In addition, Beer added a "command" neuron, which controls the activity of all the legs at once and can be used to regulate walking speed.[5]

That simple network caused the electronic insect to walk like living insects walk. When Beer and Chiel made *P. computatrix* walk at different speeds, the insect spontaneously changed the way it walked (its gait) just as real insects do. As the bug was made to walk faster, it gradually changed the way it walked from a wave gait (in which legs lift one at a time) to a tripod gait (in which balanced trios of legs alternate being off the ground).[6]

Beer and Chiel hadn't specifically programmed *P. computatrix* to change its gait as it sped up. The gait-change emerged as a consequence of the way the computer critter's nervous system was set up.[7]

Eat Like a Slug

The artificial insect's eating circuit was based on a nerve network in the primitive sea slug *Aplysia*. In the sea slug, sensory nerve cells in the gut detect hunger, and motor nerve cells control the movements of the mouth. The eating circuit in *P. computatrix* was a simplified version of the one in *Aplysia*. The circuit included just one "hunger" sensor.

When the electronic critter begins to eat, it bites its food rapidly. But as the insect becomes less "hungry," it chews more slowly and takes bites less and less frequently. That behavior, which emerged from the insect's feeding circuit, is just what living sea slugs do when they eat.[8]

But to act like a real animal, *P. computatrix* must have more than the ability to walk, eat, wander, find food, and follow walls. It also needs the sense to "know" when to eat, when to wander, and so on. In other words, the cockroach needs a way of "choosing" the right behavior at the right time, so it won't walk while it is eating, or head straight toward food when a wall is in the way.

P. computatrix does avoid such pitfalls. It appears to know what it ought to do because its nervous system is set up to produce the correct behavior in response to specific stimuli. Thus, all "decision making" emerges from the insect's artificial nervous system. The actions of *P. computatrix* may appear logical and purposeful. However, the computer critter has no sense of purpose and can't generate its own thoughts. Its actions are merely a product of the many, complex interactions of its scattered electronic neurons.

COCKROACH WANNABE! THE ROBOT

Two years into the project, Beer and Chiel decided to bring *P. computatrix* out of its computer world and into the real world in the form of a six-legged robot. This robot would use a simplified version of the nerve network that controlled *P. computatrix*: The robot would have just one of the computer critter's five behaviors—walking.[9]

Roger Quinn, the Case Western engineer recruited to design the robot, was not sure at first whether the task could be done. It is one thing for a beast to act intelligently in a computer world. It is quite another for it to survive in the real world, where forces such as gravity and friction can make things trip, fall, or fail to move at all. Nevertheless, Quinn agreed to the project.[10]

Quinn and graduate student Kenneth Espenschied constructed a six-legged, 2-pound (about 1-kg) robot out of aircraft plywood. They gave each of the robot's legs two degrees of freedom: The legs could move up and down, and backward and forward.[11]

The researchers then wired the plywood robot to a personal computer on which Espenschied had stored the walking program from *P. computatrix*. The wires were to transport sensory information from the robot to the computer, which would now

Walk like a roach. This six-legged, plywood robot walks using a program modeled after the cockroach nervous system.

receive input from the real world instead of from inside itself.

During the first tests, the robot staggered as if it were drunk, but after some fine-tuning, its gait smoothed out and it walked almost gracefully across flat, smooth surfaces. Like the artificial insect, the cockroach robot could walk at different speeds. A person could adjust its strut from about 1.8 inches per second (4.5 cm/s) to almost twice that. As the robot was made to walk faster, it automatically changed its gait just as the artificial insect did.[12]

And like the artificial insect, the robot's gait-change emerged from the wiring of its nervous system and not from programmed knowledge or instructions. The robot was walking electronic proof that principles from animal nervous systems could be used to guide electronic creatures, both in simulation and in the world.

STICK INSECT WANNABE! THE ROBOT

The Case Western team's second robot, built in 1994, is a larger, flashier, and more agile six-legged machine than the first robot. The black-and-green, 11-pound (5-kg) beast has strong legs with four degrees of freedom. Its legs can move up and down, swing back and forth, bend at a middle joint, and compress like a spring along their lengths.[13]

Like the first robot, this bigger beast is based on an animal model. It travels over flat ground like biologists believe slender, brown stick insects walk. The robot walks using a modified, electronic version of several "rules" that the German biologist Holk Cruse invented to specify how a stick insect's legs move relative to one another.[14]

The robot can walk on flat ground as fast as 3.5 inches per second (9 cm/s). As the robot is made

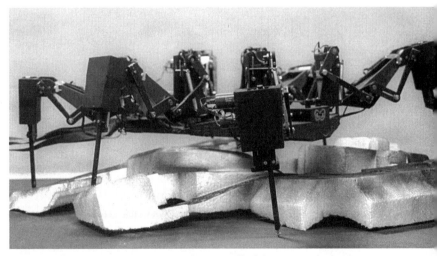

This agile robot, programmed to walk like a stick insect, negotiates the treacherous cracks and crevices of a field of Styrofoam™.

to walk faster, its gait smoothly changes from a wave gait to a tripod gait, just as happens in real stick insects. In addition, the robot can walk backwards, turn in place, and crab-walk sideways or diagonally.[15]

Balancing Acts

Like Attila and Hannibal, the new, agile robot also can walk over bumpy ground. In addition to the rules from the stick insect, the robot has animal-like reflexes that help it balance on uneven terrain.

A *postural reflex* helps the robot stay upright. If one of the robot's legs is pulled outward beyond a certain point, the robot automatically takes a step to maintain its balance. That reflex resembles a human postural reflex in which a person takes a step when a strong force tries to push him or her over.[16]

The robot also has an *elevator reflex*, which causes a foot to move backwards and then lift higher to clear the obstacle. Many animals have elevator reflexes, which cause them to step over bumps and obstacles instead of tripping over them.[17]

The robot's springy legs also contribute to its agility. The springs in the robot's legs work like the elastic tissue in mammals' legs does (see Chapter 4), to help the robot walk smoothly and efficiently. With a spring in its step, the robot saves energy and also walks smoothly, because the springs cushion the impact between its legs and the ground.[18]

With its many animal-like walking skills, the robot is one of the most agile six-legged robots ever built. It has proven its walking prowess by ambling over a field of Styrofoam™ packing material, which has lots of nooks and crannies that can trap or stick to small robot feet. Because Styrofoam™ is lightweight, it also tends to move as a robot walks over it.

Robots of the Future

In the future, Beer hopes to control a new robot with a network of simulated neurons like the network that controls the artificial insect. The robot would have all the behaviors the artificial insect has and be able to prioritize them. To create this robot, Beer plans to use the insights of Case Western biologist Roy Ritzmann, who studies cockroaches.

Beer's new robot might someday wander the Case Western University campus on its own, collecting cups, paper, and other trash, and depositing them in dumpsters. Similar animal-like robots might work in outer space to explore other planets, scour battle-fields for explosive mines, or scrub barnacles off the bottoms of ships.

For his part, Beer is more interested in making robots with survival skills than robots that can collect trash, explore planets, or perform other specific duties. He hopes his electronic creations can reveal the essence of animals' ability to adapt to their natural habitats. If he succeeds, he will create the most capable robots humankind has seen, and also gain a better understanding of how real critters survive in a cluttered and chaotic world.

CHAPTER 9

ROBOT EVOLUTION: CAN BUGBOTS BREED HUMANOIDS?

At the 1994 Robot Olympics, the tiniest robots race through a maze, each taking its turn to show off its speed and pathfinding skills. One little machine fails to reach the starting line. Another drops out after racing 0.75 inch (2 cm) in the first minute. But then, a tiny pinkish robot known as a "nanomouse" scurries through the maze in just 3 minutes, 46 seconds. Nanomouse wins the race![1]

The nanomouse is a simpleminded robot like those that inhabit Rodney Brooks's Mobot Lab at MIT. Instead of knowing where it's going, the tiny robot just uses momentary sensory input from its four antennae to issue simple orders such as "spin left" or "scoot forward." Just like the creator of nanomouse, many scientists and amateur robot builders are now patterning robots after principles that Brooks pioneered. Their robots don't think— they get around using reflexes as many primitive animals do.

Engineer Thomas Consi of MIT's Autonomous Underwater Vehicle laboratory and Jelle Atema of Boston University's Marine Program are two followers of Brooks. They are developing an 8-inch (20-cm), metal-and-plastic robot that rolls underwater and sniffs out chemicals like a lobster does. Using chemical sensors that work like a lobster's antennae, the robot follows submerged scent trails toward a scent's greatest intensity. Schools of such robot lobsters, the researchers hope, could someday trace water pollutants to their source.[2]

MICROROVERS ON MARS

Planetary scientists at the Jet Propulsion Laboratory (JPL) in Pasadena, California, have picked up on Brooks's idea of sending small robots into outer space. They've developed a series of small, wheeled robots known as microrovers designed for scooting around other planets. In fact, they have plans to send one of these rovers to Mars.

JPL's rover, which should land on the Red Planet in 1997, moves on six wheels (not legs). Larger than Cynthia Ferrell's Hannibal, it weighs 22 pounds (10 kg). However, JPL's rover uses the same insectlike reflexes that Hannibal does to get around on its own. Robots only need the smarts of an ant, claim mission planners, to do what's necessary on Mars—namely, wander around near the mother ship, snapping photos and picking up soil samples for scientists to analyze back on Earth.[3]

The new Mars rover is solar powered so it can take care of its own energy needs on Mars, but it will not be totally autonomous. Earth-bound controllers will tell the robot what tasks to perform while the robot deals with the details necessary to do those tasks. The robot can move toward an assigned destination by itself and autonomously avoid hazards along the way.

JUST HOW SMART ARE ANTS?

A robot with animal-like intelligence might be able to pick up pebbles on Mars, but could one correctly pick out items from a grocery list, checking brand names and prices? Could it understand the social conventions of waiting in line for the cashier and the intricacies of cash, credit cards, and coupons? Many scientists doubt it. They think that while simple behaviors such as "lift leg" might be important for ants and for a primitive part of human life, they have little or nothing to do with human intelligence.

Because many researchers perceive such an intelligence gap in Brooks's way of making robots, they fill that gap with the traditional approach to artificial intelligence. In other words, researchers adapt traditional robots by giving them animal-like reflexes so they can react quickly to sudden events. On top of the reflex behaviors, these robots have reasoning and mapping strategies so they can make more complex decisions. Such robotic AI hybrids are vast improvements over robots, like Shakey, that can only reason. And so the animal roboticists can also take credit for a revolution within the traditional AI community.

Revolution or no, Brooks doesn't see a need for any of the traditional stuff. He claims his behavior-based scheme alone can be used to create sophisticated robots. All that's necessary is to gradually layer more complex, goal-oriented behaviors on top of the more primitive ones—a kind of robot evolution. In this way, robots can evolve from bugbots to mousebots to dogbots to humanoids.

A Humanoid Robot

But Brooks decided he didn't have time to engineer a slow robot evolution. One day in 1993, he announced to his coworkers that he planned to stop making bugbots and would immediately begin building a humanoid, a robot whose body and brain are modeled after the human body and brain. Brooks felt it was time to prove to his critics that his theory of intelligence applies not just to simple animals and simple robots, but also to humans.

Humans are more like animals than most people believe, Brooks says. Brooks thinks the gap between human intelligence and the intelligence of say, dogs, may actually be fairly small, according to his student Cynthia Ferrell, who leads the construction of the humanoid. Brooks supposes that like animals, people use much, if not most, of their brain power to perform simple tasks such as flipping a light switch or blinking when a spit ball flies toward an eye. Not only are such behaviors important to daily life, but they are also the basis of abstract thought. Much of abstract thought, argues Brooks, develops from the day-to-day activities that provide experience.

That idea comes from modern theories about how the human brain works. Unlike traditional AI, which supposes that human reasoning is somehow separate from ordinary brain activity, many scientists now believe that human knowledge, reasoning, and even consciousness arise from the same brain cells that govern simple, everyday sensations and actions.[4]

Scattered Thoughts

Brooks is not the first person to embrace the idea that humanlike intelligence arises from simple sensation and action. However, he is the first to test that idea in a robot—an approach that has certain advantages. Unlike a human brain, a robot's brain can be freely probed and prodded. As a result, the humanoid could be experimented on in ways that a human could not be. In addition, says Ferrell, the process of building a humanlike robot may provide insights that would be difficult to get from studying humans.

The robot, named Cog, has a cubelike head with two googly eyes, a long neck, a circuit-packed, rectangular torso, and an arm. Cog will eventually have two arms and two hands for touching and moving objects, but no legs or wheels. Cog will stay put. To sense its surroundings, Cog will have cameras for eyes, microphones for ears, and skin embedded with tactile (touch) sensors. Information from all of those sensors will flow to Cog's computer "brain," which stands beside the robot like a small building shingled with circuit boards.

Although Cog's tower-of-a-brain looks nothing like the human brain, the odd electronic structure is designed to work something like its natural counterpart. Unlike computers that have one central processor and can only perform one calculation at a time, Cog's brain will carry out many operations at once, as the human brain does.

The human brain can do many things at once because it has many tiny pieces of machinery, billions in fact, in the form of nerve cells. So while one part of the brain is looking at the world, another can, say, wave a hand or tap a foot. Similarly, Cog's brain has many small electronic units called *microprocessors*, each of which has a specific duty. Some of Cog's microprocessors will process visual information; others will process sound and possibly language. Still others will coordinate body movements.

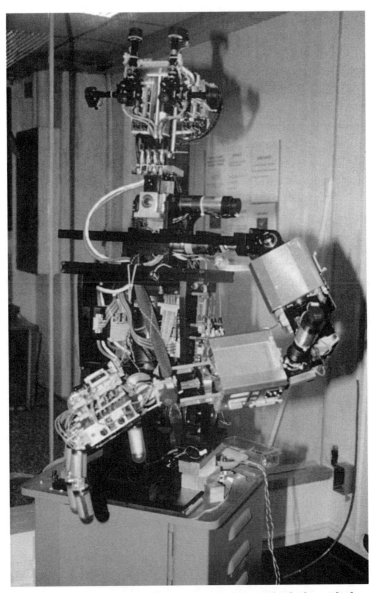

Where's my mother? Cog is wired with very little knowledge, but has the ability to learn. The humanoid's creators hope it will develop like a human infant does, perhaps even bonding with a "mother" figure.

Bringing Up Baby

In the beginning, Cog will know very little, but will be wired with the ability to learn. In that way, Cog's brain will be more like the brain of a human baby than the brain of an adult. Using its baby brain, Cog will gather, interpret, and store the information that will be constantly streaming through its senses. As it does so, Brooks, Ferrell, and Lynn Stein, another one of Cog's "parents," will anxiously watch to see how their electronic offspring develops.

If Cog develops as a human infant does, it will:

* first bat at a stationary object, and later learn to hit moving ones.
* learn to shift its eyes toward a sound, and later to move its entire head in the direction of the noise.
* bond with a "mother" figure and sometimes try to get "Mom's" attention by waving its arms.
* first display simple reflexes such as grasping any object that touches its palm, and later intentionally grasp objects and perform other actions that require some forethought.

By watching Cog develop, Brooks and his coworkers hope to gain insight into the development of human babies. For example, they would like to understand how babies figure out how to coordinate their hand movements, how they learn to interact with others, and how they begin to understand abstract concepts. Ultimately, Brooks and Stein hope that Cog will help them better understand how much of a baby's development is determined by the inevitable growth of the brain and how much depends on experience with the world.[5]

A Robot Playmate

For their part, Brooks and Stein strongly believe that intelligence is closely tied to the sensory experiences of the body—a theory called *embodiment*. According to that idea, abstract concepts will develop from everyday actions.

The researchers will study Cog closely to see if it, say, develops a sense of "up" and "down" by seeing or touching things above and below it. The researchers might also hide objects from Cog by placing them behind other objects, and then move the objects back into full view. From doing that, they could study whether Cog will learn *object permanence*, the idea that an object still exists when it is hidden from view.[6]

If Cog learns abstract concepts from sensory experience, that would be a remarkable achievement. But Brooks and Stein don't want to create an electronic introvert. They want a sociable robot, one that interacts with people. After all, most robots that think for themselves keep to themselves. And the last thing Brooks wants is a robot that in any way resembles most robots.

Cog is being groomed for a robot nursery school with a very good student-teacher ratio: one (electronic) student to many teachers. Someday, Cog's creators hope, the humanoid will "play" with its supervisors by, say, tossing a ball to them and receiving their passes. Cog might improve its technique by watching and copying its human playmates. The robot might even feel "frustrated" when it drops the ball and "happy" when a human smiles and says "good catch."

A Reason for Robots

Many researchers who study the brain are skeptical that Brooks and his team will even come close to getting Cog to think, much less feel emotions such as happiness and frustration. Why? Scientists don't know enough about how people think and feel to recreate thought and feelings in a robot. Trying to copy what we don't know, they say, is a waste of time and money.

Some scientists and engineers even go so far as to say that all projects aimed at giving a robot common sense, emotions, and people skills are wasted efforts. They argue that such a project has never succeeded and, furthermore, that humanity doesn't need robots with humanlike intelligence because people have that. People can do the work that requires general knowledge of the world and interaction with other people. Robots should stick to special-purpose jobs that they can do and that people find boring or dangerous or that require machinelike precision.

So why even try to build an intelligent robot? For one thing, it's fun. Thousands of scientists are in a thrilling race to design the smartest, most impressive robot of all. Some think the fastest path is through nature, which has evolved millions of years' worth of agile, well-adapted animals. Others have more faith in the ideas of the early AI pioneers, who believed that intelligence resides in a separate, reasoning mind that is divorced from animal-like action. Only time will tell which strategy is superior.

Yet most of the scientists in the race are also motivated by something other than fun. They have a strong desire to understand how humans and animals think and act, and believe that robots can help provide such an understanding. In addition, almost all of these researchers, no matter how they engineer intelligence, believe that smart machines with common sense, if they ever appear, would prove to be astoundingly useful. How? To paraphrase AI expert Marvin Minsky, that is like asking, "What are the uses of people?"

ROBOT
RESOURCES

Robot Organizations

The following organizations can provide information on building robots and other expert advice.

Robotic Industries Association
900 Victors Way
P.O. Box 3724
Ann Arbor, MI 48106
313-994-6088

American Association for Artificial Intelligence
445 Burgess Drive
Menlo Park, CA 94025-3496
415-328-3123

San Francisco Robotics Society of America (SFRSA)
933 Treat Avenue
San Francisco, CA 94110
415-550-0588

Association for Unmanned Vehicle Systems (AUVS)
1101 14th St. NW, No. 1100
Washington, D.C. 20005
202-371-1170

Robot Contests

Fire-Fighting Home Robot Contest
Jake Mendelssohn
Connecticut Robotics Society
190 Mohegan Drive
West Hartford, CT 06117

BEAM Robot Olympics
Mark W. Tilden
University of Waterloo
Ontario, Canada N2L 3G1
519-885-1211

SUMO Robot Competition: Contact SFRSA at the address on page 117.

The International Aerial Robotics Competition (for college students): Contact Rob Michelson at the address for AUVS, which is on page 117.

Other Robot Resources

For information on educational programs or to order robot kits, contact:

The Computer Museum
300 Congress Street
Boston, MA 02210
617-426-2800

The Franklin Institute Science Museum
Benjamin Franklin Parkway at 20th Street
Philadelphia, PA 19103-1194
215-448-1260 for course information

GLOSSARY

accelerate—to speed up.

active balance—the principle upon which fast-moving animals balance. Using active balance, a creature achieves stability on average over a short cycle of movement, such as a step, but is not stable at every moment in time.

adapt—to alter one's behavior so that one's actions are better suited to a new situation or environment.

artificial intelligence (AI)—the science of making machines exhibit behavior that would be considered intelligent if performed by a human.

automaton—a mechanical device without a computer brain that moves in lifelike ways.

autonomous robot—a mobile robot that can deal with the everyday world on its own.

binary system—a two-digit numerical system composed of 1s and 0s that is used by all modern computers.

biomechanics—the study of the physical forces that influence the shape and actions of living things.

biped—a two-legged animal or robot.

bound—a gait of a four-legged animal or robot in which the front legs act as a pair and the back legs act as a pair.

bump panel—a simple sensor that compresses when a robot bumps into something, alerting the robot to collisions.

center of mass—the point around which the weight of a body is equally distributed.

clockwork—the technology used to make old-fashioned clocks. Clockwork involves connecting various parts to cause a device to perform a precisely timed sequence of motions.

commercial robot—a robot that is sold and does useful work.

common sense—a general understanding of the world that enables people to deal with the unpredictability of everyday life.

computer simulation—a computer experiment in which electronic creatures act in an electronic world under the influence of computer-created "forces" similar to physical forces in the real world.

decelerate—to slow down.

decimal system—the 10-digit numerical system that people typically use (0, 1, 2, 3, 4, 5, 6, 7, 8, 9).

degrees of freedom—the number of ways a body part can move or rotate.

digital computer—a computer that stores all information as numbers and perform tasks by changing one set of numbers into another set.

EDVAC (Electronic Discrete Variable Automatic Computer)—the first computer to have an electronic program.

elastic strain energy—the energy stored in a compressed spring.

electricity—the energy carried by tiny, negatively charged particles called electrons.

electric motor—a motor that runs on electric current.

electromechanical tabulator—a computer that depends on both electric current and moving parts to do calculations.

electron—an elementary particle that makes up ordinary matter. Electrons are negatively charged and surround the nucleus of every atom.

electronics—a technology based on the precise control of electric current. In electronics, current is used to carry and store information.

elevator reflex—a fast, automatic action that enables an animal to step over objects.

embodiment—the theory that intelligence is closely tied to the sensory experiences of the body. According to this theory, abstract ideas develop naturally from simple actions that people perform daily.

end effector—a gripper or other tool at the end of a robot's arm.

ENIAC (Electronic Numerical Integrator and Calculator)—one of the first general-purpose electronic computers. It was developed in 1945 by John William Mauchly and John Presper Jr. at the University of Pennsylvania.

exoskeleton—an external supportive covering in some invertebrates, such as insects.

force plate—a fancy scale that measures the weight of a moving body, as well as the forward and sideways forces produced by that body.

gait—the sequence of leg motions, or stepping pattern, of an animal or legged robot.

hydraulic motor—a motor that runs on high-pressure fluid.

infrared energy—a type of electromagnetic energy that humans can't see, but can feel as heat.

integrated circuit (IC)—a solid computer chip imprinted with minute paths and regions through which current flows.

kinetic energy—the energy of motion.

laser range finder—a sensor that emits and detects a beam of energy that reflects off matter. These sensors provide robots with a rough picture of a space by directly measuring the distances to and heights of nearby objects.

linkage—a mechanism that connects parts of a machine, causing coordinated motions, such as gaits, in legged stepping machines.

microprocessor—a small electronic "brain" that performs calculations and manipulates information inside computers.

microrover—a small mobile robot.

mobot—a mobile robot.

nerve cell/neuron—one of the cells that makes up the nervous system.

nervous system—a network of interlinked cells that enables an animal to sense its environment and react to what is going on around it. In humans and other vertebrates, the nervous system includes a central brain and a spinal cord as well as peripheral sensory and motor nerve cells.

object permanence—the concept that an object still exists even after it has been moved behind another object and so is hidden from view.

pendulum—any object that hangs from a fixed point, usually on a rope or a chain, and swings freely under the force of gravity.

plug board—a board consisting of plugs, wires, and electrical sockets. A plug board held the programmed instructions of early computers.

pneumatic motor—a motor that is powered by compressed air.

postural reflex—a fast, automatic action that enables an animal to keep its body upright.

potential energy—stored energy such as that associated with altitude or height or stored in a compressed spring.

pyroelectric sensor—a sensor that detects heat.

robot—a machine with a computer brain, moving parts, and sensors.

roboticist—a scientist who creates and studies robots.

rover—a mobile robot.

R.U.R. (Rossum's Universal Robots)—a 1921 play by a Czech playwright about artificial men and women. The play introduced English-speaking people to the word "robot," which is derived from the Czech word for work.

sonar—a sensor that produces sound waves and detects their reflection off objects. In robotics, sonar is used to reveal distance and rough shape information.

static stability—the principle upon which stationary objects, such as stools, are balanced. Static stability means that at every moment in time an object is perfectly balanced.

suppress—to press down or hold back.

telepresence—a mode of operating a robot in which operators view the scene around the robot in 3-D. Telepresence creates a sense of being onboard a robot.

telerobot—a robot that receives messages via radio waves.

tendon—an elastic structure in an animal's body that connects muscles to bones.

torque—a twisting force.

traditional AI—a way of making smart machines in which computers are programmed to think like some scientists suppose people think.

transistor—a small device that controls the flow of electric current through a solid material.

tripod gait—a gait of a six-legged creature in which

a tripod of legs—the two outside legs on one side of the body and the middle leg on the other side—lift at once while the other three legs support the body.

trot—a gait of a four-legged animal or robot in which diagonal pairs of legs move together.

vacuum tube—a glass tube that contains electrodes and from which almost all the air has been removed. These tubes worked as memory units inside early computers.

SOURCE NOTES

Except where otherwise noted, all quotations come from personal interviews.

Introduction
1. Robert Kelley of Rensselaer Polytechnic Institute (Troy, New York). Telephone interview, July 1994.
2. Dr. Alvin Silverstein and Virginia B. Silverstein. *The Robots Are Here.* (Englewood Cliffs, New Jersey: Prentice-Hall, 1983), 17.

Chapter 1
1. Isaac Asimov and Karen A. Frenkel. *Robots: Machines in Man's Image.* (New York: Harmony Books, 1985), 2.
2. T.A. Heppenheimer. "Man Makes Man." *Robotics*, edited by Marvin Minsky. (Garden City, New York: Omni Press, 1985), 38, and David C. Knight, *Robotics: Past, Present, and Future.* (New York: William Morrow & Company, 1983), 23.
3. Heppenheimer. "Man Makes Man." *Robotics*, 39.
4. Asimov and Frenkel. *Robots: Machines in Man's Image.* 6.

5. Ibid.
6. Heppenheimer. "Man Makes Man." *Robotics*, 43, and Knight, *Robotics: Past, Present, and Future*, 40–41.
7. Heppenheimer. "Man Makes Man." *Robotics*, 44.
8. Asimov and Frenkel. *Robots: Machines in Man's Image*, 9–11.
9. Ibid, 11, and Heppenheimer. "Man Makes Man." *Robotics*, 55–57.
10. Heppenheimer. "Man Makes Man." *Robotics*, 57.
11. Ibid.
12. Ibid, 59–60.
13. Ibid, 60.
14. Pete Bonnasso, artificial intelligence and robotics consultant, NASA. E-mail correspondence, September 5, 1995.
15. Heppenheimer. "Man Makes Man." *Robotics*, 61–62.
16. Marty Weil. "New Competitiveness Spurs Record Robot Sales." *Managing Automation 2*, June 1994, 5.
17. Asimov and Frenkel. *Robots: Machines in Man's Image*, 13.

Chapter 2

1. William J. Broad. "Undersea Robots Open a New Age of Exploration." *The New York Times*, November 13, 1990.
2. Nemo and other "puppet" robots are not robots to some people because they can't do anything on their own. Nemo is controlled by a computer, but its real brains lie in the person commanding the computer.
3. Puppet robot is not a term roboticists use. It is a descriptive term created by the author. The same is true for the names of the other robot types in

this chapter, "stationary robots" and "coddled rovers."

4. William J. Broad. "Into the Abyss: New Robots Probe the Deep." *The New York Times*, March 9, 1993.
5. "Real Robot Captures Murder Suspect." *Current Science*, January 14, 1994, 15.
6. Ingrid Wickelgren. "Robot Explores Steaming Volcano." *Current Science*, November 4, 1994, 4.
7. Deborah Jones. "Robo-Shop." *Report on Business Magazine*, March 1994, 54.
8. Stephen Baker, "A Surgeon Whose Hands Never Shake." *Business Week*, October 4, 1993.
9. Ibid.
10. SR2 robots are made by Cybermotion Inc. of Salem, VA.
11. Jim Schlotter, head of security at the Los Angeles Museum of Art. Telephone interview, July 1994.

Chapter 3

1. The competition was held July 31–August 2 in Seattle, WA, at the annual meeting of the American Association of Artificial Intelligence.
2. M. Mitchell Waldrop. "Fast, Cheap, and Out of Control." *Science*, May 25, 1990, 959.
3. Hans Moravec. "The Rovers." *Robotics*. edited by Marvin Minsky. (Garden City, New York: Omni Press, 1985), 126–127.
4. Clive Davidson. "Common Sense and the Computer." *New Scientist*, 2 April 1994, 30.
5. Steven A. Shafer, roboticist at Carnegie-Mellon University. Personal interview, Pittsburgh, PA, April 1994.
6. Ibid.
7. Ibid.

8. Egor was built by researchers at the University of Utah.
9. Reid Simmons. Personal interview, Pittsburgh, PA, April 1994.
10. Ibid.

Chapter 4

1. Marc Raibert. "Legged Robots." *Artificial Intelligence at MIT: Expanding Frontiers*, edited by Patrick Henry Winston with Sarah Alexandra Shellard (Cambridge, Massachusetts: MIT Press, 1990), 149.
2. Ibid.
3. Ibid, 151.
4. Ibid.
5. Ibid, 153–154.
6. Marc H. Raibert and Ivan E. Sutherland. "Machines That Walk." *Scientific American*, January 1983, 44.
7. R. J. Full, M. S. Tu, and L. H. Ting. "Dynamics of Insect Locomotion Compared to Hexapod Walking Machines." *Issues in the Modeling and Control of Biomechanical Systems*, edited by J.L. Stein, J.A. Ashton-Miller, and M.G. Pandy (The American Society of Mechanical Engineers, 1989), Vol. 17, 35.
8. Raibert. "Legged Robots." *Artificial Intelligence at MIT: Expanding Frontiers,* 154.
9. John Bares. Personal interview, Pittsburgh, PA, April 1994.
10. Ibid.
11. Ingrid Wickelgren. "Robot Explores Steaming Volcano." *Current Science*, November 4, 1994, and Ibid.
12. Marc Raibert. Personal interview, Cambridge, MA, April 1994.

13. Ibid.
14. Raibert. "Legged Robots." *Artificial Intelligence at MIT: Expanding Frontiers*, 157.
15. The researchers are Rodolfo Margaria and Giovanni Cavagna.
16. Robert Full. Personal interview, Berkeley, CA, February 1994.
17. Ibid.
18. Robert J. Full. "Integration of Individual Leg Dynamics with Whole Body Movement in Arthropod Locomotion." *Biological Neural Networks in Invertebrate Neuroethology and Robots*, edited by Randall Beer, Roy Ritzmann, and Thomas McKenna (Boston: Academic Press, 1993), 5.
19. Ibid; and Robert Full. Personal interview, February 1994.

Chapter 5
1. Marc Raibert. Personal interview, Cambridge, MA, April 1994.
2. Ibid.
3. Ibid.
4. A mathematical operator that multiplies the given quantity by every lower number (integer) down to 1. For example, 4! = 4 X 3 X 2 X 1 = 24.
5. Marc Raibert, H. Benjamin Brown Jr., and Michael Chepponis. "Experiments in Balance with a 3D One-Legged Hopping Machine." *The International Journal of Robotics Research*, Vol. 3, No. 2, Summer 1984, 77.
6. Ibid; and Raibert. Personal interview.
7. Ibid, 78.
8. Marc Raibert. "Legged Robots." *Artificial Intelligence at MIT: Expanding Frontiers,* edited by Patrick Henry Winston with Sarah Alexandra

Shellard (Cambridge, MA: MIT Press, 1990), 165.

9. Ibid.
10. Jessica K. Hodgins and Marc Raibert. "Biped Gymnastics." *The International Journal of Robotics Research*, Vol. 9, No. 2, April 1990, 117.
11. Ibid, 116.
12. Ibid, 119.
13. Ibid, 123.
14. Raibert. "Legged Robots." *Artificial Intelligence at MIT: Expanding Frontiers*, 166.
15. Ibid.
16. Isaac Asimov and Karen A. Frenkel, *Robots: Machines in Man's Image* (New York: Harmony Books, 1985), 183–184. The moon is now known to have a firm, rocky surface. However, that surface is rugged and so might be most easily traversed by a legged vehicle.
17. Raibert, Brown, and Chepponis. "Experiments in Balance with a 3D One-Legged Hopping Machine." *The International Journal of Robotics Research*, 76.
18. Asimov and Frenkel. *Robots: Machines in Man's Image*, 183.
19. Raibert. "Legged Robots." *Artificial Intelligence at MIT: Expanding Frontiers,* 165.

Chapter 6
1. Robert Full. Personal interview, Berkeley, CA, February 1994.
2. Ibid.
3. Ibid.
4. Ibid.
5. R.J. Full, M. S. Tu, and L.H. Ting. "Dynamics of Insect Locomotion Compared to Hexapod Walking Machines." *Issues in the Modeling and Con-*

trol of Biomechanical Systems. edited by J.L. Stein, J.A. Ashton-Miller, and M.G. Pandy (The American Society of Mechanical Engineers, 1989), Vol. 17, 35.

6. Blickhan and Full. "Locomotion Energetics of the Ghost Crab." *Journal of Experimental Biology,* Vol. 130, 1987, 163.
7. Eight-legged ghost crabs use a pendulumlike gait when they walk like walking mammals. And, like mammals, such a gait enables the crabs to recycle much of the energy they put into walking.

Chapter 7

1. Steven Levy. *Artificial Life: The Quest for a New Creation* (New York: Pantheon Books, 1992), 275.
2. Ibid.
3. M. Mitchell Waldrop. "Fast, Cheap, and Out of Control." *Science,* May 25, 1990, 960.
4. Ibid.
5. Cynthia Ferrell. Personal interview, Cambridge, MA, August 1994.
6. Levy. *Artificial Life: The Quest for a New Creation,* 295.
7. Ibid, 295–6.
8. Ferrell. Personal interview, August 1994.
9. Ibid.
10. Richard Wolkomir. "Working the Bugs out of a New Breed of Insect Robots." *Smithsonian,* June 1991, 65.
11. Ferrell. Personal interview, August 1994.
12. Ibid.
13. Ibid.
14. Ibid.
15. Ibid.

16. Cynthia Ferrell. "Robust Agent Control of an Autonomous Robot with Many Sensors and Actuators." Master's thesis, May 1993, 72–73.
17. Levy. *Artificial Life: The Quest for a New Creation*, 282.
18. Cynthia Ferrell. Personal interview, August 1994. Rodney A. Brooks and Anita M. Flynn. "Fast, Cheap and Out of Control: A Robot Invasion of the Solar System." *Journal of the British Interplanetary Society*, Vol. 42, 1989, 478.
19. Flynn's coworkers were Rodney Brooks, Dave Barrett, and Sandy Wells.
20. Robert Buderi. "Will 'Gnat Robots' Take Wing?" *Business Week*, Innovation 1990, 56.

Chapter 8
1. Elizabeth Pennisi. "Robots Go Buggy: Engineers Eye Biology for Better Robot Designs." *Science News*, November 3, 1991, 362.
2. Ibid.
3. Ibid.
4. Randall Beer. Personal interview, Cleveland, Ohio, April 1994.
5. Randall Beer, Hillel J. Chiel, and Leon S. Sterling. "An Artificial Insect." *American Scientist*, Vol. 79, September/October 1991, 444.
6. Ibid, 449.
7. Ibid.
8. Ibid, 451.
9. Pennisi. "Robots Go Buggy: Engineers Eye Biology for Better Robot Designs." *Science News*, 362.
10. Ibid.
11. Randall Beer. Personal interview, April 1994.
12. Kenneth Espenschied. Personal interview, Cleveland, Ohio, April 1994.

13. Ibid.
14. Randall Beer. Personal interview, April 1994.
15. Ibid.
16. Ibid.
17. Ibid.
18. Kenneth Espenschied. Personal interview, April 1994.

Chapter 9
1. Joshua Mills. "At Robot Olympics, the Battle of the Nanomice." *The New York Times*, March 8, 1994.
2. David L. Chandler. "Robotic Lobsters." *Technology Review*, February/March 1994, 10.
3. Faye Flam. "Swarms of Mini-Robots Set to Take on Mars Terrain." *Science*, Vol. 257, September 18, 1992, 1621.
4. Rodney A. Brooks and Lynn Andrea Stein. "Building Brains for Bodies." *Massachusetts Institute of Technology Artificial Intelligence Laboratory Memo*, No. 1439, August 1993, 2.
5. Cynthia Ferrell. Personal interview, Cambridge, MA, August 1994.
6. Ibid.

BIBLIOGRAPHY

(Items marked with an asterisk are recommended for further reading.)

Aleksander, Igor and Piers Burnett. *Reinventing Man: The Robot Becomes Reality.* (New York: Holt, Rinehart and Winston, 1983).

*Asimov, Isaac and Karen A. Frenkel. *Robots: Machines in Man's Image.* (New York: Harmony Books, 1985).

Baker, Stephen. "A Surgeon Whose Hands Never Shake." *Business Week*, October 4, 1993.

Bares, John. Personal interview, Pittsburgh, PA, April 1994.

Beer, Randall, Hillel J. Chiel, and Leon S. Sterling. "An Artificial Insect." *American Scientist*, Vol. 79, September/October 1991, 444–452.

Beer, Randall, Hillel J. Chiel, and Leon S. Sterling. "A Biological Perspective on Autonomous Agent Design." *Robotics and Autonomous Systems*, Vol. 6, 1990, 169–186.

Beer, Randall. Personal interview, Cleveland, Ohio, April 1994.

Berger, Fredericka. *Robots: What They Are, What They Do.* (New York: Greenwillow Books, 1992).

Blickhan, Reinhard and Robert J. Full. "Locomotion Energetics of the Ghost Crab." *Journal of Experimental Biology,* Vol. 130, 1987, 155–174.

*Bortz, Fred. *Mind Tools: The Science of Artificial Intelligence.* (New York: Franklin Watts, 1992).

Broad, William J. "Into the Abyss: New Robots Probe the Deep." *The New York Times,* March 9, 1993.

Broad, William J. "Undersea Robots Open a New Age of Exploration." *The New York Times,* November 13, 1990.

Brooks, Rodney A. "Intelligence Without Reason." *Massachusetts Institute of Technology Artificial Intelligence Laboratory Memo,* No. 1293, April 1991, 1–27.

Brooks, Rodney A. "New Approaches to Robotics." *Science,* 253, September 13, 1991, 1227–1232.

Brooks, Rodney A. and Anita M. Flynn. "Fast, Cheap and Out of Control: A Robot Invasion of the Solar System." *Journal of the British Interplanetary Society,* Vol. 42, 1989, 478–485.

Brooks, Rodney A. and Lynn Andrea Stein. "Building Brains for Bodies." *Massachusetts Institute of Technology Artificial Intelligence Laboratory Memo,* No. 1439, August 1993, 1–15.

Buderi, Robert. "Will 'Gnat Robots' Take Wing?" *Business Week,* Innovation 1990, 56.

Bylinksy, Gene. "High Tech Help for The Housekeeper." *Fortune,* November 2, 1992, 117.

Chandler, David L. "Robotic Lobsters." *Technology Review,* February/March, 1994, 10.

Chapuis, Alfred and Edmond Droz. *Automata: A*

Historical and Technological Study. (Neuchatel, Switzerland: Editions du Griffon, 1958).

Crawford, Robert J. "Machine Dreams." *Technology Review*, February/March 1994, 77–79.

Davidson, Clive. "Common Sense and the Computer." *New Scientist*, 2 April 1994, 30–33.

Espenschied, Kenneth. Personal interview, Cleveland, Ohio, April 1994.

Ferrell, Cynthia. Personal interview, Cambridge, MA, August 1994.

Ferrell, Cynthia. "Robust Agent Control of an Autonomous Robot with Many Sensors and Actuators." Master's thesis, May 1993.

Flam, Faye. "Swarms of Mini-Robots Set to Take on Mars Terrain." *Science*, Vol. 257, September 18, 1992, 1621.

Full, R.J, M.S. Tu, and L.H. Ting. "Dynamics of Insect Locomotion Compared to Hexapod Walking Machines." *Issues in The Modeling and Control of Biomechanical Systems*, edited by J.L. Stein, J.A. Ashton-Miller, and M.G. Pandy. (The American Society of Mechanical Engineers, 1989, Vol.17), 35–39.

Full, Robert, J. "Integration of Individual Leg Dynamics with Whole Body Movement in Arthropod Locomotion." *Biological Neural Networks in Invertebrate Neuroethology and Robots*, edited by Randall Beer, Roy Ritzmann, and Thomas McKenna. (Boston: Academic Press, 1992) 3–20.

Full, Robert. Personal interview, Berkeley, CA, February 1994.

*Harrar, George. *Radical Robots: Can You Be Replaced?* (New York: Simon & Schuster, 1990).

Hodgins, Jessica K. and Marc Raibert. "Biped Gymnastics." *The International Journal of Robotics Research*, Vol. 9, No. 2, April 1990, 115–132.

Jones, Deborah. "Robo-Shop." *Report on Business Magazine*, March 1994, 54–62.

*Jones, Joseph L. and Anita Flynn. *Mobile Robots: Inspiration to Implementation*. (Wellesley, Massachusetts: A K Peters, 1993).

*Knight, David C. *Robotics: Past, Present and Future*. (New York: William Morrow & Co., 1983).

*Levy, Steven. *Artificial Life: The Quest for a New Creation*. (New York: Pantheon Books, 1992).

*Lewin, Roger. "Birth of a Human Robot." *New Scientist*, 14 May 1994, 28.

Mills, Joshua. "At Robot Olympics, the Battle of the Nanomice." *The New York Times*, March 8, 1994.

*Minksy, Marvin (ed.) *Robotics*. (Garden City, New York: Omni Press, 1985).

Pearson, Kier. "The Control of Walking." *Scientific American*, December 1976, 72–86.

*Pennisi, Elizabeth. "Robots Go Buggy: Engineers Eye Biology for Better Robot Designs." *Science News*, November 3, 1991, 361–363.

Raibert, Marc. "Legged Robots." *Artificial Intelligence at MIT: Expanding Frontiers*, edited by Patrick Henry Winston with Sarah Alexandra Shellard. (Cambridge, Massachusetts: MIT Press, 1990), 149–179.

Raibert, Marc, H. Benjamin Brown Jr., and Michael Chepponis. "Experiments in Balance with a 3D One-Legged Hopping Machine." *The International Journal of Robotics Research*, Vol. 3, No. 2, Summer 1984, 75–92.

*Raibert, Marc and Ivan E. Sutherland. "Machines That Walk." *Scientific American*, January 1983, 44–53.

Raibert, Marc. Personal interview, Cambridge, MA, April 1994.

"Real Robot Captures Murder Suspect." *Current Science*, January 14, 1994, 15.

"The Robot Game Show Script: Version 8." The Franklin Institute, Philadephia, PA, November 15, 1990.

*Rosheim, Mark E. *Robot Evolution: The Development of Anthrobotics.* (New York: John Wiley & Sons, 1994).

Shafer, Steven A. Personal interview, Pittsburgh, PA, April 1994.

Silverstein, Alvin, Dr. and Virginia B. Silverstein. *The Robots Are Here.* (Englewood Cliffs, New Jersey: Prentice-Hall, 1983).

Simmons, Reid. Personal interview, Pittsburgh, PA, April 1994.

*Skurzynski, Gloria. *Robots: Your High-Tech World.* (New York: Bradbury Press, 1990).

Travis, John. "Building a Baby Brain in a Robot." *Science*, 264, May 20, 1994, 1080–1082.

Waldrop, M. Mitchell. "Fast, Cheap, and Out of Control." *Science*, 248, May 25, 1990, 959-961.

Wickelgren, Ingrid. "Robot Explores Steaming Volcano." *Current Science*, November 4, 1994, 4–5.

*Wolkomir, Richard. "Working the Bugs out of a New Breed of Insect Robots." *Smithsonian*, June, 1991, 65–73.

"World's Smartest Johnnymop." *Popular Mechanics*, June 1993, 22.

INDEX

Active balance, 62, 74
    speed, 68, 83
Adapting, 50–53
Aiken, Howard, 19
Alexander, R. McNeil, 64
Angle, Colin, 91, 94
Animals, 44–45, 52–53
    balance, 61–62, 64
    eating circuit, 102
    insect studies, 80–81
    movement, 54, 60–61,
        67–68
    recognition, 90
Artificial beings, 13
Artificial intelligence (AI),
    44–45
    animals as models, 44–45,
        52–53, 67–68
    hybrids, 110
    Shakey, 45–47
Asimov, Isaac, 27
Atema, Jelle, 109
Automatons, 15–16, 17
Autonomous robots, 43

Babbage, Charles, 17, 19
Balance, 61–62, 106
    pogo-stick robot, 68–71
    running, 67
Bardeen, John, 22
Beer, Randall, 98–102
    future, 107
Behavior-based robots, 88–91,
    110
Binary system, 21
Binnard, Michael, 84–85
Biomechanics, 81
Bouncing, 70–71, 81–82
Brain, 10, 11
    humanoid, 113
    multiple, 88–90, 91–92
Brattain, Walter, 22
Brawn, muscle, 11–12
Brooks, Rodney, 86–90, 95,
    110, 111–115
Bugbots, 91–93, 108
Bump panels, 49

Capek, Karel, 25

Center of mass, 61
Chiel, Hillel, 99, 100, 102
Clockwork, 15
Cockroaches, 78–81
 computer, 99–100
 how they run, 81–83
 locomotion, 94, 101
 robots, 84–85, 103–104
Coddled rovers, 29, 37–39
Commercial robots, 39
Common sense, 47–48
Computers, 17, 19
 robot brain(s), 11, 88–90,
  91–92
 simulation, 84
Connell, Jon, 90
Consi, Thomas, 109
Contests, 118
Cruse, Holk, 105

Decimal system, 21
Definition of robots, 9
 in this book, 13–14
Degrees of freedom, 11, 103,
 105
de Vaucanson, Jacques, 16, 17
Devol, George C., Jr., 22
Digital computers, 17, 19

Eating circuit, 102
Elastic strain energy, 64
Electricity, 19
Electric motors, 12
Electronics, 19–21
Elevator reflex, 106
Embodiment, 115
Emotions, 115–116
End effector, 11
Energy, 62–63, 64–65
Engelberger, Joseph, 14, 22
Espenschied, Kenneth, 103
Evolution, 108, 110

Exoskeletons, 80

Factory robots, 11, 22–23, 25,
 35–37
"Father of robotics", 14
Ferrell, Cynthia, 94, 111
Firby, James, 42
Flynn, Anita, 95, 97
Force plates, 81
Full, Robert, 71, 78–83

Gymnasts, robot, 73–74

Hodgins, Jessica, 71
Hollerith, Herman, 19
Hospitals, 36–37, 38–39
Humanoid robot, 111–115
Hydraulic motors, 11

Independent robots, 39–40
Industrial robots, 22–23
 PUMAs, 25
 stationary, 35–37
Infrared energy, 49
Insects, 78–79. See also Cockroaches
 behavior-based, 88–89
 computer simulation, 84
 movement, 80–81
Integrated circuit (IC), 24
Intelligence, 41–43
 embodiment, 114–115
 mobile robots, 25
 scattered thoughts,
  111–113
 tradition AI, 44–45

Jacquard, Joseph Marie, 17
Jacquet-Droz, Pierre, 16

Kelley, Robert, 39
Kilby, Jack, 24

Kinetic energy, 64
Kits, to order, 118
Koechling, Jeff, 71

Laser range finders, 49
Laws of Robotics, 27
Legged machines, 55–56
  eight legs, 60
  four legs, 74–75
  future use, 76
  limitations, 60–61
  one leg, 68–71
  six legs, 56–60
  two legs, 71–73
Linkage, 56

Machine tools, 10
Mauchly, John William, 21
McGee, Robert, 58, 67, 68
McLurkin, James, 97
Microprocessors, 113
Miniature robots, 97
Minsky, Marvin, 116
Mobile Robotics Competition, 41, 50
Mobile robots, 29, 37–39
Moondozers, 87
Moravec, Hans, 88
Mosher, Ralph, 56
Motor skills, 52

NASA (National Aeronautics and Space Administration), 95
Nervous system, 99, 100–101
Newell, Allen, 45
Noyce, Robert, 24

Object permanence, 115
Organizations, 117

Parts of a robot, 11–12

Pearson, Kier, 94, 101
Playmates, 114–115
Plug board, 21
Pneumatic motors, 11
Postural reflex, 106
Potential energy, 63–64
Presper, John, Jr., 21
PUMAs (Programmable Universal Machines for Assembly), 25
Puppet robots, 29–35
Pyroelectric sensors, 93

Quinn, Roger, 103

Raibert, Marc, 66–77, 84
Recognizing robots, 13–14
Redefining robots, 13
Reflexes, 108
  animal, 90–91
  AI hybrids, 110
  elevator, 106
  postural, 106
Remote-control, 29–30
Resources, 117–118
Rhythm generator, 101
Ritzmann, Roy, 107
Roboticist, 13
Running, 66–67, 70–75
  cockroaches, 81–83
  gymnast, 73–74

Science fiction, 25–27
Seifert, H., 76
Senses, 48–49
Sensors, 11, 49–50, 93
Sensory experience, 114–115
Shakey, robot, 25, 45–47
Shockley, William, 22
Simmons, Reid, 50
Simon, Herbert, 45
Simpleminded robots, 86–87

Size, 94–95, 97
Sonar, 49
Speed, 61–62, 76–77
  and balance, 68, 83
  insects, 78
Spy bug, 95–96
Static stability, 61
Stationary robots, 35–37
Stein, Lynn, 114, 115
Stick insect robot, 105–106
Stepping machines, 55–56
Stepping patterns, 68
Sutherland, Ivan, 58

Telepresence, 32, 34–35
Telerobots, 29–30
"Thinking skills", 11
Throwaway robots, 97
Tinbergen, Niko, 90
Transistors, 22, 24
Tripod gait, 82

Unimates, 22–23

Vacuum tubes, 20–21

versus transistor, 22
Virtual legs, 74
Vision, 48
von Neumann, John, 21

Waldon, Kenneth, 58
Walking robots, 54–55, 94
  cockroach, 103–104
  the first, 91–93
  like a bug, 101–102
  stick insect, 105–106
Weaving loom, 17, 18
Wilson, Donald, 57
Working robots, 12–13
  control strategies, 29
  crime, 30–31
  hospitals, 36–37, 38–39
  mowing lawns, 37
  patrolling, 38
  police aid, 30–31
  space exploration, 32–35,
    86–87, 95, 109–110
  undersea, 28, 30
  in volcanoes, 32

ABOUT THE AUTHOR

Ingrid Wickelgren
was born in Boston,
Massachusetts, but
grew up in Eugene,
Oregon. She received
a biology degree from Stanford
University. Although she has
written articles on a wide variety of science-related
topics for magazines including *Discover*, *Health*,
Business Week, *Parenting*, and *Popular Science*, this
is her first book for children. She is a member of the
National Association of Science Writers and the
New York Road Runner's Club. She currently lives
in Brooklyn, New York.